Developing Spiritual Growth in Junior High Students

Ray Johnston

ZondervanPublishingHouse
Grand Rapids, Michigan

A Division of HarperCollins*Publishers*

El Cajon, California

Developing Spiritual Growth in Junior High Students

Copyright © 1994 by Youth Specialties

Youth Specialties Books, 1224 Greenfield Drive, El Cajon, California 92021

Edited by Sharon Stultz

Cover design, interior design, and typography by Jamison Bell Advertising

Printed in the United States of America

ISBN: 0-310-49041-3

94 95 96 97 98 / ML / 6 5 4 3 2

YOUTH SPECIALTIES BOOKS

Professional Resources
Advanced Peer Counseling in Youth Groups
Called to Care
The Church and the American Teenager
    (Previously released as Growing Up in America)
Developing Student Leaders
Feeding Your Forgotten Soul
Help! I'm a Volunteer Youth Worker!
Growing Up in America
High School Ministry
How to Recruit and Train Volunteer Youth
    Workers (Previously released as Unsung
    Heroes)
Junior High Ministry (Revised Edition)
The Ministry of Nurture
Organizing Your Youth Ministry
Peer Counseling in Youth Groups
The Youth Minister's Survival Guide
Youth Ministry Nuts and Bolts
110 Tips, Time-Savers, and Tricks of the Trade

Discussion Starter Resources
Amazing Tension Getters
Get 'Em Talking
High School TalkSheets
Junior High TalkSheets
More High School TalkSheets
More Junior High TalkSheets
Option Plays
Parent Ministry TalkSheets
Tension Getters
Tension Getters Two

Special Needs and Issues
The Complete Student Missions Handbook
Divorce Recovery for Teenagers
Ideas for Social Action
Intensive Care: Helping Teenagers in Crisis

Ideas Library
Ideas Combo 1–4, 5–8, 9–12, 13–16, 17–20,
    21–24, 25–28, 29–32, 33–36, 37–40, 41–44,
    45–48, 49–52
Ideas Index

Youth Ministry Programming
Adventure Games
Creative Bible Lessons on the Life of Christ
Creative Programming Ideas for Junior High
    Ministry
Creative Socials and Special Events
Good Clean Fun
Good Clean Fun, Volume 2
Great Fundraising Ideas for Youth Groups
Great Games for City Kids
Great Ideas for Small Youth Groups
Greatest Skits on Earth
Greatest Skits on Earth, Volume 2

Holiday Ideas for Youth Groups (Revised Edition)
Hot Illustrations for Youth Talks
Hot Talks
Junior High Game Nights
More Junior High Game Nights
On-Site: 40 On-Location Youth Programs
Play It! Great Games for Groups
Play It Again! More Great Games for Groups
Super Sketches for Youth Ministry
Teaching the Bible Creatively
Teaching the Truth About Sex
Up Close and Personal: How to Build Community
    in Your Youth Group

4th–6th Grade Ministry
Attention Grabbers for 4th-6th Graders
4th–6th Grade TalkSheets
Great Games for 4th-6th Graders
How to Survive Middle School
Incredible Stories
More Attention Grabbers for 4th-6th Graders
More Great Games for 4th-6th Graders
More Quick and Easy Activities for 4th-6th Graders
Quick and Easy Activities for 4th-6th Graders
Teach 'Toons

Clip Art
ArtSource™ Volume 1—Fantastic Activities
ArtSource™ Volume 2—Borders, Symbols,
    Holidays, and Attention Getters
ArtSource™ Volume 3—Sports
ArtSource™ Volume 4—Phrases and Verses
ArtSource™ Volume 5—Amazing Oddities and
    Appalling Images
ArtSource™ Volume 6—Spiritual Topics
Youth Specialties Clip Art Book
Youth Specialties Clip Art Book, Volume 2

Video
Edge TV Volumes 1–9
Next Time I Fall in Love Video Curriculum
Promo Spots for Junior High Game Nights
Resource Seminar Video Series
Understanding Your Teenager Video Curriculum
Witness

Student Books
Going the Distance
Good Advice
Grow for It Journal
Grow for It Journal Through the Scriptures
How to Live with Your Parents Without Losing
    Your Mind
I Don't Remember Dropping the Skunk, But I Do
    Remember Trying to Breathe
Next Time I Fall in Love
Next Time I Fall in Love Journal
101 Things to Do During a Dull Sermon

Dedication

This book is affectionately dedicated to Jon and Joan Archer:

I heard about Christ at church . . . but met Him in your home.

I heard about commitment in sermons . . . but saw it in your marriage.

I learned about ministry in seminary . . . but experienced it in your lifestyle.

Your authenticity, passion, loyalty, and generosity attracted me (along with scores of others) to Christ, to costly commitment, and to real-life ministry. The investment you made in me has made all the difference—thanks!

Contents

Foreword

Spiritual growth in junior highers.

Really?

Not many think it's possible. Most people hold to the view that when kids hit junior high or middle school, they take a giant step backward when it comes to spiritual things. They don't grow; they shrink. To find spiritual growth in a junior higher, you need a microscope, they say.

Okay, I admit it's hard to believe that kids who throw paper wads from the church balcony during Communion are making progress, but in some mysterious way they most certainly are. With junior highers, growth generally follows the path of regression. Things tend to get worse before they get better.

But you'll read all about that in this book, and a lot more besides. Ray Johnston believes as I do that the most significant spiritual growth of all happens during the early adolescent years, when kids are shedding the trappings of childhood religion and putting on the new clothes of adult faith. It is most often during the junior high years when students make the important decisions that shape their future values and beliefs.

And in today's world, if you wait around too long to help kids make good decisions about the important things in life, you'll miss the boat. Ask anyone who works with the high school crowd these days: they are essentially doing rehabilitation work.

You want to help your junior high kids grow spiritually? You've come to the right place. This book contains a lot of good stuff to help you achieve that goal. But as you use the excellent material on the pages that follow, I'd like for you to keep a couple of things in mind.

First, forget results. What I mean is—don't count on being able to measure the spiritual growth that is taking place in the lives of your junior highers with any degree of accuracy. Junior high kids will defy any standard that you impose upon them. They are sometimes going forward, sometimes going backward, but nearly always—they will disappoint you. Don't expect them to act like little adults. They will not.

Spiritual growth in junior highers can only be measured by youth workers who have learned the fine art of patience. Wait a decade or so. If you give your kids some time, chances are you'll end up with some young adults who will be eager to thank you for being there for them during their crucial early adolescent years. Remember that the call to junior high ministry is a call to faithfulness, not to success.

Second, forget programs and methods. In other words, don't depend on the stuff in this book to turn your kids into spiritual giants. Ultimately, junior high ministry is relational. You know the old saying, "much more is caught than taught." Double that with junior highers. The best thing we can do to insure spiritual growth in junior highers is to surround them with good people—caring adults who love kids and who love Jesus.

Ray Johnston is someone like that. He loves kids; he loves Jesus. No wonder so many of the students who have passed through his youth groups over the years are now following in his footsteps—loving kids and loving Jesus too!

—Wayne Rice

Acknowledgments

THROUGH HIS ENTHUSIASM AND EXAMPLE Wayne Rice has shaped junior high ministry in America perhaps more than anyone—

by believing in ministry to younger kids (before any of us wanted any part of it);

by giving the better part of the last three decades to training and motivating adults to give themselves to junior highers;

and by faithfully staying at it.

Wayne has helped move junior high ministry from the shadows to the mainstage of youth ministry.

Much of the material in Chapters One and Three originated with a seminar written by Wayne and led by the Youth Specialties seminar team. I am grateful for his permission to use the material.

I am also thankful for the team of people at First Covenant Church in Sacramento who faithfully serve behind the scenes. Special thanks to LaRee Hauschild and Robin Canfield for typing until all hours of the night. My thanks also go to Joan Hibbs, Ilene Perryman, Jan Dinen, Claudia Clowes, and Lois Heath who answer too many phone calls, deal with too many interruptions, and work with such dedication and grace that it is actually fun to walk into the office.

I am grateful for the editing skills and friendship of Noel Becchetti. Thanks, Noel, for the investment of time and your willingness to go the second mile, which turns writing into ministry.

Special thanks also go to Jeff Koons and Bob Gaddini for their valuable assistance as sounding boards in developing the strategy in this book.

Finally, I remain amazed by the patience and support of my family during the writing process. To my wife Carol, and kids, Mark, Scott, Leslie, and Christy—thank you for your patience, love, endurance, and support. You are the greatest!

Defining Spiritual Growth
for Junior High Students

The Case for Junior High Spiritual Growth

THE MOST COST-EFFECTIVE PROGRAM *in any church is a strong junior high department. Junior high school is now the make-it-or-break-it time for children, in my opinion. Why? Because this is when peer pressures really take hold. Our best efforts and budgeting need to be aimed at doing a good job with kids in this age bracket.*

No more important step exists for any church than to develop a highly visible, highly effective junior high program that will reach significant numbers of boomer kids. Toward that end, an effective starter strategy for your church will be to gather all your junior high workers together and show them how vital they are, not only in the evangelization of the children, but also to the wider purpose of reaching, through the children, their parents and communities.

—From *The Baby Boomerang*
(Regal, 1990) by Doug Murren

VETERAN YOUTH WORKER, WAYNE RICE, tells the following story about a student in his youth group named Steve: Steve was one of those kids in my junior high group who improved my prayer life by merely showing up. When he first came to our junior high group, he showed little interest in spiritual things. He was a constant source of trouble for me and the other youth leaders. He made me long for an easier ministry, like being personal chaplain to Saddam Hussein. His compelling need to show off earned him the nickname "Spittoon"—his favorite trick was to spit up into the air, then catch his spit in his mouth. He had a sharp tongue, never paid attention to anything we were teaching, and I daily asked God to transfer his dad to Siberia.

But for some reason, I felt that God was calling me to make Steve a special project. I decided that I would take "Spittoon" under my wings and disciple him—claim him for the kingdom of God. I worked hard to establish a good relationship with him. After several weeks of building relational bridges with Steve, I asked if he would be interested in participating in our Junior High Disciples study course. To my surprise, he said yes. At first, I wondered if this was such a good idea. Due to his penchant for showing off and drawing attention to himself, he was having a negative impact on the other students. But after a few weeks, I noticed a change. He started bringing his Bible to class. He started to participate in the singing and the discussions. Almost miraculously, his attitude seemed different.

Six months into the program, he was quoting Scripture in class and leading the group in prayer. Steve's parents came to me and said that they were amazed at the progress we had made with him. He was doing his household chores, getting good grades at school, and spending time every day in personal devotions.

But the greatest moment of all for me was when Steve, after having been involved in Junior High Disciples for only fourteen months, came to me and said that because of my ministry in his life, God had called him into full-time Christian ministry. I began literally jumping up and down for joy. About that time, my wife woke me up and told me to quit dreaming because I was shaking the bed.

WAKE-UP CALL

Steve doesn't exist, of course. But the junior high students in your group do, and there is a growing sense among youth workers that the number one priority in terms of time, programming, relationships, and effort needs to be in junior high ministry. Waiting until high school to challenge kids to spiritual growth in today's world can be too late. Unfortunately, most churches major on high school ministry while junior high ministry remains a largely untapped gold mine.

I'm convinced that, for maximum youth ministry impact, nothing equals the development of a good junior high ministry. Let me share some reasons why.

Junior high students are available. Recently, I was talking with some youth workers about barriers to spiritual growth that we ran into with our kids. We covered all of the typical things: peer influence, partying, drugs, sexual temptation, media, culture, hymnals. But we all agreed that the single biggest barrier was busyness, especially among high school students. The days of taking all our high school students on a weekend retreat are over. There are football games, clubs, tests, work, family outings; you almost need commuter flights to get the youth group together. A couple of us joked about paying kids to come to the youth group just to get everyone together. But think about it: junior high students are simply more available than high school students.

First, they are too young to get jobs. Studies show that 65 percent of high school students work. Few, if any, junior high students do. Secondly, junior high school students have what I call P.D.L.—Pre-Drivers License Syndrome. Most junior high students are at the stage in life where they are dying to get out of the house and will go anywhere any interested youth worker is willing to drive them.

Effective youth ministry requires availability, because it takes time for a kid to get to know you, to trust you, and to sense your values. It takes time to help kids discover that God loves them. It takes time to help a teenager learn the implications of following Christ. The group of students with the most amount of time available are junior highers.

Junior high students are teachable. Psychologist Stephen Glenn describes the process of maturing from childhood to adulthood (the teenage transition years) in three stages. One stage is called discovery and takes place roughly between ages twelve to fourteen. Puberty has just hit junior highers, and the physical, intellectual, social, and emotional changes that accompany this change of life create a growing awareness in these kids that a whole new adult world is opening up to them. This discovery phase produces three effects in the life of a junior higher:

Rapid experimentation. Junior high kids will try anything! It's called discovery by experimentation. Whether it's smoking, drinking, dating, driving, or bungee jumping off the roof of the church, you can bet junior high kids will experiment with it. Experimentation is one of the primary ways junior highers discover who they are and what they like and dislike. From lifestyles to clothing styles, junior highers are going to try it on for size.

A thirst for information. Junior highers are full of questions. Their antennae are on full alert. Junior high kids are like gigantic sponges, soaking up information. They have tremendous questions about themselves, their faith, their future, and their worth.

A sense of transition. The junior high years are a time of transition. They remind me of the trapeze artist who has just let go of one trapeze but hasn't connected with the other. Junior highers are leaving

CHAPTER ONE

childhood, but are not ready to arrive at adulthood. Insecurity, a sense of searching, and a desire for change are common during this time as kids begin to make major decisions about who they will become.

Each of these *effects* provides us with unique opportunities for ministry to junior highers:

Because junior highers desire *experimentation*, they will try *anything!* Junior high kids are simply more open than they will be at the high school level. Junior high specialist and author Wayne Rice confirms this when he states, "Senior high students, by comparison, are nearing the completion of this process and will often be extremely rigid and set in their ways."[1] In contrast, junior high students are willing to listen and experiment. Unchurched junior highers are usually willing to come and try out a Christian youth group. Many youth workers believe that the most open group to the Gospel is junior high students.

Because junior highers desire *information*, they are open to *teaching*. A tremendous amount of spiritual growth can occur in junior high students because they want information, even about their faith. They don't think they know it all, and the teacher who is open to discussion and questions can have a great time teaching the truth to junior high kids.

Because junior highers are experiencing *transition*, they are open to *change*. Ministry is often most effective during times of transition. Whether it is students entering college, a couple entering marriage, a couple becoming parents, or kids entering the junior high years, people are most open to new input, growth, and change during times of transition. The junior high years embody the greatest transition that most people will ever experience, childhood to adulthood. The opportunities this transition creates for life-changing ministry requires more, not less, of our resources and involvement.

Junior high students are open. During my "honeymoon" period of youth ministry (which lasted about the length of one Sunday school lesson), I came to the rude awakening that *the number one factor in students' openness to my influence was their age.* Spiritual growth requires openness, trust, and responsiveness on the part of students. But age is a determining factor in the openness and responsiveness of students to our friendship, leadership, and programs. The age/openness breakdown usually looks like this:

High school seniors: Usually unresponsive. They have reached the

16

top, have their relationships and values pretty well in cement, and are usually separating from the youth ministry (and their parents) as they focus on their future.

High school juniors: Somewhat unresponsive. They are still impressed with the "old" youth pastor and the idea of developing loyalty to someone new is not high on their agenda. Most of the juniors in my last youth ministry had already determined their convictions, relationships, and preferences, and the idea of someone new coming in and shaking up their world caused resistance rather than responsiveness.

High school freshmen and sophomores: Much more responsive, especially to a new youth worker who takes them seriously (they will be amazed that anyone does) and takes the time to involve them in designing and developing the ministry.

Junior high students: Highly open and receptive to both relationship building and creative programming. The phrase "the old youth worker didn't do it that way" (which I regularly heard from high school students) was never echoed by the junior highers. In a new youth ministry, junior high students will be the first on board . . . the first to get excited . . . the first to bring their friends . . . and the first to follow your leadership. For youth workers just starting out, giving high priority to junior high may bring greater and quicker results.

Junior highers are growing up fast. *Fast Times at Ridgemont High* are rapidly becoming *Fast Times at Ridgemont Junior High.* Books like *Too Old Too Soon* by Doug Fields (Harvest House, 1991) and *All Grown Up and No Place to Go* by David Elkind (Addison-Wesley, 1984) make a compelling case that kids are reaching puberty sooner, growing up faster, and making major life decisions earlier than at any time in history.

Some of the decisions now faced, and often made, in junior high include the following:

- Will I have sex or not?
- Will I drink alcohol or not?
- Will I use drugs or not?
- Will I cheat or not?
- Will I believe in God or not?
- Will I go to church or not?

CHAPTER ONE

Changes in the family, the influence of the media, a shift in parenting styles, and rapid changes in cultural values mean that junior high students are bombarded with decisions at an age that just a few short years ago would have been unthinkable. Adolescent medicine specialist Dr. Victor Strasburger states:

"Short of being in a war, these are the most dangerous times that adolescents have ever had to face. There are now more choices that teenagers have to make, and less guidance to make those choices. Now, fourteen and fifteen year olds need to decide, 'Am I going to have sex or not? Am I going to smoke pot or not? Am I going to drink or not?' "[2]

Two generations ago, these types of decisions were made in college. A generation ago, they were made in high school. Now they are being made in junior high.

Junior high students are needy. Today's world extracts a heavy price from kids. Having their values shaped by media bombardment, alienated from their parents and other adults, crammed into overcrowded classes, victims of a culture they didn't create but are often blamed for, young people have been left to fend for themselves.

Ron Hutchcraft, Youth for Christ director in New York City, calls teenagers in the last four decades the Lost Generation. He notes:

In the 1950s teenagers lost their *innocence*. Liberated from their parents by music, movies, cars, and money, they were faced with a brave new world of freedom without the accompanying moral guidelines that could lead to healthy choices.

In the 1960s they lost their *authority figures*. Kids were told to trust no one over thirty. Young people were robbed of trusting relationships with adults whose wisdom and experience could have proven to have been a great benefit.

In the 1970s they lost their *love*. The "Me Decade" was dominated by a focus on self. Families and values came apart, and American teenagers, starving for love, settled for sex.

In the 1980s young people lost *hope*. Stripped of their innocence, authority, and love, teenagers stopped believing in the future and began living as if there wouldn't be one.

As Christians, we are called to minister to the "least of these" (Matt. 25:45). Often these are junior highers. Abandoned by our culture and manipulated by our media, they are eager for even one adult to step into their lives and make a difference.

CHAPTER ONE

Junior high students will become high school students. A solid investment in junior high students will have a dramatic impact on your high school ministry. Let's be honest: one reason we don't prioritize junior high ministry is the lack of visible results. Because junior high is a time of transition, many of our students won't "arrive" spiritually to the extent that high school students will. But there is hope: these same kids will become high school students. Launching a growing junior high ministry is much easier than launching a high school ministry, and within two years, your high school group will grow as waves of junior high graduates arrive.

Recently, while speaking at a youth ministry workshop, I was asked what I would do differently if I were just starting out in my first youth ministry. The answer came easily: I would do the exact opposite of what I did in my last youth ministry, which was to focus on high school and delegate the responsibility for junior high ministry to others. *I now believe the best way to build a growing high school ministry is not to focus on high schoolers, but to make a major investment in junior highers and patiently allow that to impact the high school ministry.*

Take any two youth workers starting at the same time. Have one invest all his or her time in high school ministry, with the other focusing on junior high. Each youth ministry grows for the next four years. But not only will the youth worker focusing on junior high have a vital ministry, he or she will send waves of kids into a rapidly-growing high school ministry every year.

Best of all, most of these incoming students will be the future leaders of the high school ministry, having developed spiritual maturity during their junior high years. What an incentive to motivate us to pour our lives into the spiritual development of our junior high students!

Endnotes

1. Wayne Rice, *Junior High Ministry* (El Cajon, Calif.: Youth Specialties, 1987), 21.
2. Strasburger quoted by Jamie Rugless, "Being There" (Young Life fund-raising letter, 1992).

Junior High Discipleship: Overcoming the Oxymoron

BACK IN MY BACHELOR DAYS, my three roommates and I ran a junior high ministry at a small church in Duarte, California. We were completely untrained. None of us had a background in youth ministry, recreation, psychology, or hand-to-hand combat, all of which would have come in handy. We made every mistake in the book, and probably invented some new ones. None of us even had a church background—which as I look back on it, came in handy in one way: *No one told us that junior high students couldn't or wouldn't take God seriously.* We were so naive that it simply never occurred to us that junior high students wouldn't want to become disciples.

Our little youth ministry took off like a shot (of course, it's easy to double the size when you start with two). Kids in the community came to Christ in increasing numbers. Over a three-year period, new kids came to Christ at nearly every one of our Wednesday evening outreach events. Students started taking spiritual growth seriously. Students began carrying and actually reading Bibles. We started junior high support groups and pretty soon had six Bible studies going, many at the request of students. We saw kids fall in love with God and with each other.

Now, these kids weren't perfect. We had all of the cliques, mishaps, adventures, breakups, runaways, zits, peer pressures, and inconsistencies that occur in any group of junior highers. But kids got involved, loved God with all their hearts, and took their commitment to Christ seriously.

For too many Christians, the term junior high disciple ranks up there with oxymorons like jumbo shrimp, unemployment benefits, and mini-sermon. As a result, we have bought into some major misconceptions about spirituality and adolescence:

Misconception #1: Junior highers are not able to be effective disciples. They are not ready to worship, study, learn, or serve.

Misconception #2: Junior highers are not ready to take God seriously. To expect any ministry from them is unrealistic and self-deluding.

Misconception #3: Junior highers are the "church of tomorrow." They are not capable of being in the services, taking the offering (they might *really* take it!), or serving in leadership positions.

Misconception #4: Junior highers don't like being with adults.

Misconception #5: Junior highers are not interested in learning.

PERCEPTION IS REALITY

When we buy into these misconceptions, it's easy to ignore junior high ministry because we are convinced that the potential for real growth isn't there. However, that is all a matter of our perspective.

Bruce Wilkinson, president of Walk Thru the Bible Ministries, discovered the power of perception during his first year of teaching. A new Bible professor at a Christian college, he was to teach three sections of the same Bible class. On the way to teach Section II, he was informed that this class was different from his others. Each year, the college placed the sharpest, brightest students in Section II to build a new set of student leaders for the school.

The minute he walked into the class, he could tell they were a "cut above." During the next few weeks their work was better. Their assignments were turned in sooner. And their test scores averaged at least one grade above the other two classes.

Halfway through the semester, the dean of the college asked Wilkinson what he enjoyed most about his new teaching position. His reply was immediate as he described the thrill of teaching Section II: better student responsiveness, higher test scores, etc. The dean interrupted to gently inform him that the Section II concept had been stopped the previous year. The brightest students were now spread evenly throughout all three classes.

Wilkinson ran back to his office and pulled out his grade book. The evidence was startling. Section II's grades averaged one grade higher as a class. Their papers were better. Their attendance was better. The lesson was clear. Three separate classes had the same texts, same assignments, same professor, same tests, same lectures—with only one variable: the teacher's perception of the capabilities of the respective classes. The problem with junior high spiritual growth may not be a lack of potential on the part of the kids, but a lack of perspective on our part.

CHAPTER TWO

How can we correct the misconceptions we may have about the potential of junior highers? By recognizing and affirming three "positive perspectives" about junior high students.

Junior high students are ready to grow spiritually. Junior high students are more ready to grow spiritually than many adults are ready to enable that growth.

First, junior highers are highly impressionable, much more so than high school students. Something happens to most kids upon entering high school; they become "too cool for life." High school students are often too cool for God, for their parents, for the youth worker, for most adults, and for most of the students in the youth group. The great thing about most junior high kids is that they aren't "cool" yet. Many are still hero worshipers. Whether it's the hottest new rock star on MTV or the latest speaker at youth camp, junior high kids are open to, and usually impressed with, any caring adult who is willing to step into their lives.

I have noticed that after I speak at a high school conference, I have to initiate conversations with kids. At a junior high conference, kids will flock around me and are much easier to talk with. Also, junior highers are making major decisions in many areas of their lives, as we discussed in Chapter One. They are ready to consider a decision to follow Christ, and most are willing to follow through with that decision.

Recently, my wife, Carol, and I had dinner with two of our best friends, Jesus and Melissa Arcienega. Both became Christians in our little junior high ministry years ago. They continued to walk with God through high school and college, and are now married. What a joy it was to have them and their new son in our living room. Every time we see those two, it serves as a great reminder that junior high students are ready to grow spiritually.

Junior high students are willing to grow spiritually. When you successfully tap in to the enthusiasm of a junior high group, you can light up a city. Ministry is fun because junior highers are literally up for anything! The great thing about this age-group is that you can get them so excited that they will just about go through a wall (you have to go first, but they will follow).

Junior highers in the stage of discovery are outward looking, risk taking, idealistic, and adventurous. Whether it's bungee jumping, toilet papering the senior pastor's house, river rafting, or starting an on-campus Bible study, these kids will try it if you are personally enthusiastic.

CHAPTER TWO

Take Abbey Loorz, for example. This seventh-grade girl recently stood up in front of seven hundred other junior high students at an evangelistic beach rally and talked openly about her faith in Christ and the impact He has had on her life. Or Keven Meier, a seventh grader who started a weekly Bible study in his school, which he prepares and leads. Within three months, Kevin had twenty-five students attending his study.

Junior high students are able to grow spiritually. Some years ago at a family conference, I asked a father of four how he had raised such capable kids. I nearly keeled over when he told me that one of the rituals they had as a family occurred when their kids arrived in eighth grade. At the start of their last year of junior high school, each of his kids was given all of the responsibility for handling the family finances. They paid the bills, cashed the checks, handled the investments, the whole banana. He could tell that I was shocked. He said, "Kids are much more capable than we think. They just need someone in their life that believes that."

Not only are students ready and willing to grow spiritually, they are able to do so. They are capable of worship. Some of the deepest and most emotional worship experiences I've ever had have been with junior highers in a camp setting. They are capable of significant friendships. They are capable of serving and making an impact.

A couple of years ago, while working on a week-long mission trip in Mexico, I had to drive one of our kids to Palm Springs due to a family emergency. What a contrast! In a few hours, we went from a setting where thousands of students, many of them junior highers, were giving their lives away in Mexico to Palm Springs, where we ran into thousands of teenagers partying in the streets, burning cars, and destroying the town.

As I drove back to Mexico after leaving the student with her family and again observed the vitality, enthusiasm, and passion in the lives of these young servants, I gained a new appreciation for the ability of junior high kids to impact their world for Christ.

THEY CAN DO IT

There is little doubt that junior high students are ready, willing, and able to grow spiritually. The real question is this: Are we ready, willing, and able to help them grow?

What Is Real-Life Junior High Spiritual Growth?

A GROUP OF STUDENT LEADERS at our small church in Duarte, California, had decided to do a series of junior high outreach breakfasts. The first three ran pretty smoothly. The students did a great job of programming, the promotion was excellent, and the breakfasts grew from the original two students to over one hundred. For the fourth breakfast, their gala Christmas celebration, one of the students dressed up like Rudolph the Red-Nosed Reindeer for a Christmas skit.

During the skit, "Rudolph," in typical show-off style, jumped up on one of the tables and began to dance around, making reindeer-like noises (whatever those are). Suddenly, "Rudolph" slipped on one of the plates and crashed down on the table. The antlers strapped to his head severely gored a junior high kid in the forehead. Fifteen minutes later, I was at the hospital trying to explain to the doctor and the injured kid's parents how this kid got gored by Rudolph the Red-Nosed Reindeer at our church breakfast.

HEADS UP!

Real-life junior high ministry is like the story of the cross-eyed discus thrower: he didn't set too many records, but he sure kept the crowd awake. Trying to understand real-life junior high spiritual growth has all of the comfortable feel of a casual stroll through a mine field. One minute you are speaking to one hundred unchurched kids and sensing that God is working, and the next you are at the hospital with a victim of a clumsy red-nosed reindeer.

Which is the real junior high ministry? Both. Junior high kids have one rapidly developing foot in the adult world and another still in the past. Junior high students can and do grow spiritually, but this growth can look very different from the growth of people at a more "settled" stage of life.

Junior high spiritual growth is marked by some important characteristics that, as we are able to recognize them, can help us to

CHAPTER THREE

understand what God is doing in these young lives. Veteran junior high ministry specialist Wayne Rice has outlined five characteristics that help to define real-life discipleship for junior highers:

Real-life spiritual growth for junior highers is appropriate. In a recent issue of *Leadership Journal,* Roberta Hestenes, president of Eastern College, was asked this question: "What exactly is spiritual maturity? What does it look like?" She answered, "Maturity is engaging in behavior that is appropriate to the stage in which you are. A four year old is mature when he or she does everything it's reasonable for a four year old to do. We don't consider a four year old immature because he or she can't do what a twelve year old does. But if he or she doesn't do the things four year olds are capable of, then he or she is immature. So one definition of maturity is living up to the capacities God has made possible for you."[1]

What this means for junior highers is that their signs of growth are mixed with inconsistent (that is, appropriate for junior highers) behavior. Junior high students will memorize Scripture one minute and get into a fight the next. What we can do is give them room for growth and expect ups and downs.

As David Elkind states, "Young adolescents are able to conceptualize fairly abstract rules of behavior, but they lack the experience to see their relevance to concrete behavior."[2] It is normal for a junior higher to say one thing and to do another. What appears to be hypocritical to us is actually a step forward for them. Wayne Rice details the reason for this apparent hypocrisy when he says, "Junior highers have not yet developed the ability to relate theory to practice, or faith to works."[3]

A junior high group recently studied world hunger. Then, when given the choice to spend the money they had raised on themselves or the hungry, they decided to spend the money on themselves. While this can be discouraging, it is normal. They will learn to connect belief with behavior as they grow older. As you know, we all keep learning that lesson throughout adulthood. The junior higher is just starting out.

Real-life spiritual growth for junior highers is transitional. Some of the greatest transitions take place during the junior high years. Physically, intellectually, socially, emotionally, and spiritually, the junior higher is making a monumental transition from childhood to adulthood.

During this period of transition, a junior higher is much like the trapeze artist suspended in midair, flying from one trapeze to the next without a safety net. Because they are going through rapid change and have their feet firmly planted in midair, we can expect a heavy combination of insecurity and transition.

This may mean that not all of our junior highers will "arrive" spiritually. It is not unusual to have a group of junior highers excited about serving in Mexico and completely indifferent to serving at home. It is also quite normal for junior highers to make great commitments at camp and "chop" each other down during the bus ride back.

As we mentioned in Chapter One, psychologist Dr. Stephen Glenn describes junior highers as being in the discovery stage of life. He notes that junior highers are trying everything on for size. While they are tremendously open to spiritual growth, this openness is combined with disorientation and confusion as they make the transition from childhood thinking and reasoning to more adult ways of functioning.

Real-life spiritual growth for junior highers is experiential. Speaking at the 1988 Youth Specialties National Youth Workers Convention in Chicago, David Elkind said, "Junior high students should not be required to go to school at all. They should instead be allowed to go somewhere and build a boat."

Junior highers learn much more by doing than by hearing or reading information. If they are building a boat, a house for a homeless family, performing in a musical, or even playing games, they will learn more about life and values than by sitting in a classroom.

Emphasize experiential spiritual-growth activities with your junior highers, and go light on the traditional classroom-oriented approach. You'll be much more effective.

Real-life spiritual growth for junior highers is practical. Junior high discipleship relates to the world that the junior higher is familiar with. Memorizing the minor prophets will not mean much to the kid who is having major problems making friendships. Doing Bible study with junior highers is great; however, care needs to be taken that it relates to their world.

If we want to nurture spiritual growth in junior highers, our kids will need experiences and content at their level. I have had better luck helping junior highers study the Bible than teaching Bible studies. Taking my junior highers to a soup kitchen and letting them serve dinner is always more effective than lecturing on servanthood. Practical

CHAPTER THREE

Bible studies like "How to Use Your Mouth" or "How to Build Friendships" draw attention, interest, and have more of an impact because of their relevance to the kids' world.

Real-life spiritual growth for junior highers is relational. Junior high school principals agree that the best teachers—the ones who get the best results—are also the teachers the students like the best. In California, the school system spent $10 million to improve the reading curriculum in the junior high schools. After a period of testing, they found that the new curriculum was no better than the old as long as the teachers remained ineffective.

The quality of your junior highers' spiritual growth will be directly proportional to your getting adults with them who really like the kids for who they are. We will talk more about this important principle in Chapter Four, but it is important to note that if you are a person who loves and relates well to junior highers, almost any curriculum will be fine.

HOSANNAS AND HORSERADISH

When I was in college, my three roommates and I were involved in a junior high ministry. One weekend we invited several of the "leadership-type" seventh grade guys over to spend the night. We had a great evening of sports, pizza, Bible study, and prayer. I went to bed that evening feeling great about the spiritual growth taking place in these young, committed kids. The next morning, this feeling was confirmed when I heard a knock on my door and in walked the eight young disciples serving us *breakfast in bed*. Feeling like the youth workers of the year, we dove into the pancakes. One bite into the meal, we knew something was wrong. Our seventh grade disciples had carefully put horseradish and mustard between the pancakes. We spat the pancakes out and reached for the Pepto-Bismol just in time to see these eight future spiritual giants rolling on the floor in laughter.

That is the world of junior high discipleship: hosannas and horseradish. Great commitments and immature inconsistency. Compassion and cruelty.

Real-life junior high spiritual growth is three steps forward and two back. But that puts you ahead of where you were. Junior high spiritual growth is appropriate, transitional, experiential, relational, practical, and for those willing to take the risk, attainable!

CHAPTER THREE

Endnotes

1. Roberta Hestenes, "Can Spiritual Maturity Be Taught?" *Leadership Journal* (Carol Stream, Ill.: Christianity Today, Inc., Volume IX Number 4, 1988), 14.

2. David Elkind, *All Grown Up and No Place to Go* (Reading, Mass.: Addison-Wesley, 1988), 43.

3. Wayne Rice, *Junior High Ministry* (El Cajon, Calif.: Youth Specialties, 1987) 134.

Creating Opportunities
for Healthy Relationships

We loved you so much that we were delighted to share with you
not only the gospel of God
but our lives as well.

—The apostle Paul,
a first-century youth worker

CHICAGO THUNDERSTORMS ARE LEGENDARY. In our old house, they always had the same effects—knocking out the power and causing our little son Mark to race down the hall and jump into our bed. One night in particular, I heard his feet hit the floor about one second after I heard the crack of thunder. As he dove headlong into our bed and snuggled up to me, I could feel him shaking. Wanting to get some sleep, I gently tried to talk him into returning to his bed. He was adamant. There was no way he was going back to his bed. Finally, I called on my trump card, our golden retriever, Captain. I asked him if being in his bed would be okay if I let Captain sleep with him. He rolled over, put his arms around me, and said, "No way! I want someone with me that has lips and can talk!"

SOMEONE TO WATCH OVER ME

Junior high kids are usually a little more subtle, but if we listen carefully, we can hear the same desire for someone who will be there for them during the storms of adolescence. The storms of change and the rolling thunder of insecurity combine to produce a great need for healthy relationships.

Unfortunately, at the time of life in which they most need relationships, they are often the most isolated. Encouraging relationships are absent at school. The average junior high campus is a self-image war zone. A friend of mine had someone write this in his junior high yearbook:

"God created rivers,
God created lakes,
God created you,
Everyone makes mistakes."

31

CHAPTER FOUR

Encouraging relationships are seldom found with teachers. The size of the average American class keeps growing, and overburdened teachers struggle just to cope, without the time to build relationships.

Encouraging relationships are seldom found at home. In 1940, the average American home had eight hours of conversation per day. Now it is roughly fourteen minutes per day, of which 12.5 minutes is negative, one-way communication.[1]

Encouraging relationships with significant adults are seldom found in church. Teenagers are one of the most segregated groups in society. They are with other teenagers at school, at work, in sports, and in clubs. Unfortunately, the minute we get them in a church setting with potential for all kinds of great relationships with adults, we segregate them into the junior high room, never to be heard from again.

This lack of encouraging relationships, especially with adults, has two results. First, teenagers become susceptible to peer pressure in proportion to the lack of quantity and quality time with significant adults. Secondly, most teenagers have no clue what they want to be when they grow up because they have never spent time with adults, learning about the potential options available to them.

If junior high students are going to start down the path to significant spiritual growth, the key to that journey will be the consistent presence of one adult. As Robert Vieniega states in his book *A Gift of Hope* (Little, Brown, 1985), "Almost without exception, those who survive a tragedy give credit to one person who stood by them, supported them, and gave them a sense of hope."

QUALITIES FOR HEALTHY RELATIONSHIPS

Whatever level our junior highers are at spiritually, the need for caring relationships remains consistent. The question then becomes, What qualities are needed in adults to build healthy relationships with junior highers? The following six qualities are especially valuable:

Adults who can affirm. Youth speaker and author Mike Yaconelli, speaking at a Youth Specialties 1993 Resource Seminar, described an environment that would enable growth in any junior high kid when he declared, "What if young people grew up in a world where they were wanted? What if they grew up in a sea of expectation where they were saturated with hopes and visions and possibilities? What if everyone around them was eager to listen, eager to teach, eager to spend time, eager to converse, eager to contribute to their character? What if young people grew up in an atmosphere in which everything they did mattered? Where people cared enough to say no? What if young people were loved unconditionally, not only allowed to fail but encouraged to fail? What if young people grew up in a world where mistakes were seen as necessary, where shortcomings were seen as the other side of 'longcomings?' What if young people were exposed to the winds of risk so they could experience the exhilarating feeling of real self-worth? What if young people were surrounded by laughter and embraced by the strong arms of unconditional love?"

Every junior high kid has the inalienable right to have someone excited about him or her. I began the Christian life because of a friend, Jim Schibsted, who loved me. I grew spiritually because of the consistent support of a teacher in our community, Jon Archer, who consistently communicated that he believed in me. I continue to be excited about ministry through the encouragement of a group of guys who continue to surround me, support me, and walk together with me in service.

Adults who can listen. The average junior higher is talked at by her parents, taught at by his teachers, yelled at by her coaches, and preached at by his youth workers—and no one is listening.

The junior high years are filled with intense and conflicting feelings, and junior highers usually deal with their feelings in one of three ways:

They will take them out on themselves, their parents, their youth workers, and their teachers; they will hold them in; or they will talk them out with a trusted friend.

A listening adult is a gift from God for a junior higher—a trusted friend who can help them talk through and work through their feelings in healthy ways.

Adults who can invest their time. Some of you reading this book will feel inadequate to minister to junior highers because all you can invest is an hour per week. Invest it! By investing even one hour per week, you can make a difference in the life of a relationally-starved junior higher.

In my last church, we had a teenager devastated by a divorce that she never saw coming. One of our volunteers set up a weekly breakfast with her just to keep in touch. At the end of the year, this young girl stood in front of our congregation during a student sharing time. There wasn't a dry eye in our church as she broke down and said, "My parents divorced this year. If it weren't for Suzanna having breakfast with me each Wednesday, I'm not sure I would be here today."

Something is always better than nothing. Whether it's breakfast, shopping, leading a Bible study, or having the students over to do your laundry, any time you can give to kids will be worth it.

Adults who can have fun. The last person any junior higher wants to be around is an adult who is uptight and rigid. Junior highers want to be with adults who can laugh at life and at themselves. In junior high ministry, the possibilities for this type of laughter are continually present. Veteran youth worker Dave Veerman lists some "Murphy's Laws."

1. If something can spill, it will.
2. The projector bulb will burn out.
3. The printed announcement will always have an important typo.
4. Half of the kids will not know about the meeting—they didn't get the mailer, get called, or see the announcement in the bulletin.
5. When you give junior highers a paper to keep, they will lose it in less than ten minutes.
6. Surefire icebreakers always bomb.
7. When you fill up every minute of your meeting (in your planning), everything will take longer than you expected.
8. When you already have gaps in the meeting (in your planning), everything will go more quickly than you expected.[2]

Some of the best modeling we will ever do for kids is to stay loose and have fun. Kids are amazed that adults can actually have a good time. It blows the stereotypes they have of "church people," and creates an openness for developing relationships. Author and speaker Brennan Manning sums it up best: "If you have the joy of the Lord in your heart, please notify your face."

Adults who can pray. In twenty years of youth ministry, I have yet to meet a volunteer who was as effective in reaching, nurturing, and developing junior highers as Bill Laffin. He was like a junior high Pied Piper. Kids flocked to Bill, loved to hang out with him, endured his Bible studies, went to any camp he was at, and usually developed a lasting relationship with God.

All of this was rather surprising because Bill had none of the stereotypical qualities of a naturally gifted junior high youth worker. Yet year after year, Bill's ministry to junior high students flourished.

Finally I asked him what his secret was. How was he so effective when so many were having so little impact? Bill pulled a small notebook out of his dresser and said, "It's all in here." At the top of each page was the name of a student. Under the kid's name was a small snapshot of the kid with a description like "Jimmy is from a broken home, not doing well in math, and likes the Lakers." At the bottom of each page was a list of prayer requests for that student and his or her family. Every morning during his quiet time, Bill Laffin would pull out his notebook and pray for his kids. Many of them have never "recovered" from his ministry of prayer.

Prayer may be the most underestimated weapon in our youth ministry arsenal. Prayer unlocks the power of God in our lives, gives us renewed confidence for our kids, and shapes the way we minister to them.

Adults who can help kids through the tough times. Everyone who watched the 1992 Olympics was deeply moved by the story of Derek Redmond. Running for Great Britain, he made it to the semi-finals of the mens' 400-meter race. About one hundred yards from the finish line, Redmond pulled a hamstring muscle and fell in agony to the track surface. His hopes for a medal were crushed. As concerned officials ran to help Derek off the field, he waved them away. The pain must have been excruciating; but there, in front of millions of people, Derek Redmond did the unthinkable. He slowly pulled himself to his feet and began to hop to the finish line. Suddenly, there was a commotion in the crowd. A man pushed his way onto the track. The man was Jim Redmond, Derek's father. He ran onto the field and grabbed his son. He said to Derek, "You don't have to do this, son." Derek replied, "I have to finish." So his dad said, "We started this together; we are going to finish this together." And with the arms of his father around him, Derek Redmond made it to the finish line.

For too many junior highers, the "wonder years" are really the "blunder years." Many of the kids you minister to are injured. Some have fallen. Some are in pain. Helping junior highers grow spiritually begins with relationships. It means coming out of the stands, putting your arms around a kid, and saying, "We started this together; we are going to finish this together."

Helping kids grow spiritually is to help them begin to walk with Jesus. Programs will help. Teaching will help. Games will help. Retreats will help. But the only way to help them begin that process is to put your arms around your students and walk with them. They may not end up in the Olympics, but they will never "recover" from your impact on their lives.

Endnotes

1. Joe White, *Looking for Leadership* (Branson, Mo.: Operation Challenge).

2. Veerman, Dave, *Reaching Kids before High School* (Wheaton, Ill.: Victor, 1990).

Building Spiritual Growth into Junior High Students

Developing a Plan for Junior High Spiritual Growth

I N THIS CHAPTER, I AM GOING TO GIVE YOU A PLAN that will enable you to design effective programs for the wide variety of kids in your ministry. We'll do this by covering the following five steps:

1. Evaluate your students' spiritual levels

2. Set your goals

3. Develop your game plan

4. Anticipate what you hope to achieve

5. Develop "gateways" to lead students to further growth

1. Evaluate your students' spiritual levels. Junior high kids range on an amazing spiritual spectrum—from some who are spiritual to kids who carry chain saws to Sunday school. In developing an effective plan for fostering spiritual growth in your junior highers, it will help to get a clear focus on where your students are in relationship to their spiritual life.

Almost every student in your youth group is going to fall into one of the following three categories:

CASUAL KIDS: READY TO VISIT

These students may be visiting for the first time or may be attending regularly. They may be churched or unchurched. These kids may be there because your outreach ministry attracted them or because their parents have bribed (or forced) them. These are kids who have not yet become followers of Jesus. I remember Michael, a seventh grader who was in and out of our junior high ministry. If the event involved food and fun, he was the first student through the door, but the minute he sensed a Bible study coming, he could disappear in a flash. If you've got casual kids like this (and who doesn't), don't let it get you down. The great thing is that they are there! Pray for them and develop outreach programs to continue to attract them.

Chapter Six gives you strategies and programs to attract students at this level. Outreach ministry is exciting because of its potential for impact. Many of the unchurched junior highers in your community will respond to a good outreach program, and some of your casual junior highers may be only one meeting away from starting a relationship with Christ and becoming ready to grow.

CURIOUS KIDS: READY TO GROW

These are the junior high students who have started a relationship with Christ and are interested in spiritual growth. In twenty years of junior high ministry, I have yet to see a *whole* group of junior highers at this level. However, almost all groups have some students who have responded to Christ and are ready to grow spiritually.

Chapter Seven provides you with programs to foster spiritual growth in these students. In terms of the chart found on page 104, kids become Christians when they move from casual to curious. They may still have a ton of questions, and inconsistency is part of their experience, but they have started down the path to spiritual growth.

COMMITTED KIDS: READY TO SERVE

Committed junior highers are the kids in your group who are ready to serve (not students you would like to have committed). Chapter Eight gives you ways to get your students involved in missions and service. Developing opportunities at this level allows students to discover that their lives count, and that they can make an impact for the kingdom of God right now.

You will be using the material in Chapters Six, Seven, and Eight to plan programs to meet the needs of these students. But the first step in developing your plan is to identify where your kids fall in the three categories. Figure One on page 41 shows you how you can do this. Later in this chapter, using an expanded version of this chart, you can write in the names of your kids in the box you feel best describes where they are at spiritually.

A well-rounded junior high ministry will develop ministries to reach each type of student. Helping junior highers grow spiritually requires getting them to first enter the growth process, and then to help them journey from casual to committed.

FIGURE ONE

JUNIOR HIGH STUDENTS		
CASUAL KIDS	CURIOUS KIDS	COMMITTED KIDS
Ready to Visit	*Ready to Grow*	*Ready to Serve*
Tony Collins	*Scott Oas*	*Clark Crebar*
Randy Edens	*Randy Phillips*	*Jeff Koons*
Kim Larson	*Wally Coots*	*Darrell Sarmento*
Mark Johnston	*Evelyn Johnson*	*Leslie Johnston*
Paul Larsen	*Scott Johnston*	*Dave Fredricksen*
Jay Hall	*Gary Gaddini*	*Cindy Clark*
	Arsenio Lettermen	*Christy Johnston*
		Dave Leno

If a student is currently not attending, we can design outreach ministries to attract that student to visit our youth group. If a student is attending but showing little interest, we can create a thirst for spiritual growth and develop spiritual growth activities that will enable that kid to grow in his or her walk with God. If a student is growing spiritually, we can create service opportunities for that student to actively serve God.

2. Set your goals. Establishing your goals will help you focus on growth areas for your students and how to make that growth happen. Setting a goal for the casual student could be as simple as increasing attendance at your next outreach event, while the goal for the curious student might be giving kids a positive view of the Bible. In Chapters Six, Seven, and Eight, I have listed several possible goals in each of these areas. The key is to set positive goals that will maximize your students' opportunities for growth in their areas of need.

3. Develop your game plan. Every junior high ministry is unique, requiring its own game plan. In Chapters Six, Seven, and Eight, you'll find programming ideas that you can mix and match to suit your game plan. If your focus is outreach, you may spend most of your time using the ideas in Chapter Six. If your concentration is developing spiritual growth, Chapter Seven will provide solid game plan ideas. When you are ready to develop a game plan that challenges kids to serve, Chapter Eight will be the most helpful.

For a game plan to be effective, it needs to have three components. First, you need a *relational* component. This is critical, because people reach people. I'm always amazed when I ask adults who were in my junior high ministry what changed their life. The answer is always a relationship.

Secondly, you need a *conceptual* component. Learning is an important part of junior high ministry, and creatively helping junior highers understand their faith is essential.

Third, you need an *action* component. Experience is the best teacher, particularly with junior highers who crave action.

I have put the game plan components in this order for a reason. Traditionally, youth ministry has started from the conceptual component, which gives junior highers a sense that the church is a "cold," unfriendly place where they are taught but not loved. Traditional youth ministry has also stopped short of giving junior highers the chance to serve, which leaves kids feeling bored and useless. Putting together a game plan that includes all three components will create an atmosphere and provide opportunities that will maximize your kids' possibilities for growth.

The game plan structure in Chapters Six, Seven, and Eight utilizes these three components. Whether you are working on outreach, spiritual growth, or service, you can mix and match ideas selected from each of these components. I've distributed these ideas where they seem to fit best; however, many of these ideas can fit into more than one category. Use the ideas that will best meet the goals you have set for your students.

4. Anticipate what you hope to achieve. Focused programming, with specific goals in mind, has high potential to produce tangible results. In the next three chapters, I have listed specific results that you could expect to gain in each of the three areas of focus. Take time to envision the results you hope to achieve through your programs. This will enable you to focus your strategies and pray more intelligently. You will know what you hope to gain, and you will minister to kids with a sense of anticipation.

5. Develop "gateways" to lead students to further growth. The most fulfilling part of my experience in youth ministry has been seeing kids actually grow spiritually. Having unchurched kids visit for the first time, watching casual students catch fire spiritually, and praying with junior high kids as they make commitments to serve God energizes me and keeps me going.

CHAPTER FIVE

Junior high spiritual growth is helping kids discover gateways from where they are now to a new stage of spiritual growth. Helping students move to a new stage of growth can be exciting, exhausting, thrilling, frustrating, and breathtaking. I have sometimes been moved to tears, occasionally moved to my knees, and often moved to my tiptoes in anticipation of what some of these kids are becoming.

In Chapters Six, Seven, and Eight you'll find ideas you can use to provide your kids with gateways that will enable them to progress down the path to spiritual maturity. Figure Two illustrates this principle:

FIGURE TWO

JUNIOR HIGH STUDENTS		
CASUAL KIDS	CURIOUS KIDS	COMMITTED KIDS
GATEWAYS →	GATEWAYS →	
Ready to Visit	*Ready to Grow*	*Ready to Serve*

PLANNING WORK SHEETS

As you move ahead into Chapters Six, Seven, and Eight, look over the ideas for each of the three types of ministries, the possible goals, game plan ideas, possible results, and "gateway" ideas. Then, use the work sheets found on pages 44–52 to develop your long-range plan and individual programs.

Long-Range Planning Overview—Students
(Goals—Game plan—Gains—Gateway)

1. Write in the names of your students at the level of their spiritual growth.

MY STUDENTS		
CASUAL KIDS	CURIOUS KIDS	COMMITTED KIDS
Ready to Visit	*Ready to Grow*	*Ready to Serve*

Long-Range Planning Overview—Goals
(Goals—Game plan—Gains—Gateway)

2. Set your goals. With the students' needs in mind, write in your goals for each area of your junior high ministry.

MY GOALS		
CASUAL KIDS	CURIOUS KIDS	COMMITTED KIDS
Ready to Visit	*Ready to Grow*	*Ready to Serve*

Long-Range Planning Overview—Game Plan
(Goals—Game plan—Gains—Gateway)

3. Develop your game plan. Based on your goals, write your game plan ideas for each area of ministry.

GAME PLAN IDEAS		
CASUAL KIDS	CURIOUS KIDS	COMMITTED KIDS
Ready to Visit	*Ready to Grow*	*Ready to Serve*

Long-Range Planning Overview—Gains
(Goals—Game plan—Gains—Gateway)

4. Anticipate your gains. Write in what you expect to gain from your programs in each area.

GAINS		
CASUAL KIDS	CURIOUS KIDS	COMMITTED KIDS
Ready to Visit	*Ready to Grow*	*Ready to Serve*

Long-Range Planning Overview—Gateway
(Goals—Game plan—Gains—Gateway)

5. Develop your gateways. What ideas and programs do you want to use to build bridges for further growth?

GATEWAY IDEAS		
CASUAL KIDS	CURIOUS KIDS	COMMITTED KIDS
Ready to Visit	*Ready to Grow*	*Ready to Serve*

Programming Calendar

6. Schedule your game plan. Develop a programming time line that includes your game plan and gateway ideas.

PROGRAMMING YOUR FIRST SEMESTER				
	SEPTEMBER	OCTOBER	NOVEMBER	DECEMBER
Outreach Programs				
Spiritual Growth Programs				
Service Programs				

CHAPTER FIVE

Programming Calendar

PROGRAMMING YOUR SECOND SEMESTER					
	JANUARY	FEBRUARY	MARCH	APRIL	MAY/JUNE
Outreach Programs					
Spiritual Growth Programs					
Service Programs					

CHAPTER FIVE

Programming Calendar

PROGRAMMING YOUR SUMMER				
	JUNE	JULY	AUGUST	EARLY SEPTEMBER
Outreach Programs				
Spiritual Growth Programs				
Service Programs				

CHAPTER FIVE

The following form will enable you to plan out each programming event incorporating the ideas in Chapters Six, Seven, and Eight.

Program Planning Work Sheet

Program _____ Target Group _____ Date_____

1. List the kids you are expecting will attend this event.

CASUAL KIDS	CURIOUS KIDS	COMMITTED KIDS
Ready to Visit	*Ready to Grow*	*Ready to Serve*

2. Fill out the program planning sheet.

EVENT COMPONENTS	SCHEDULE FOR THE EVENT		
GOALS 1. *Write in your goals for the event.*	PROGRAM 5. *Write in your program using your event components.*		
		MATERIALS NEEDED	PERSONNEL
	Prep/Setup		
	Opening		
GAME PLAN 2. *Write in your game plan ideas for the event.*	Game Plan		
GAINS 3. *Write in what you hope to achieve.*	Response		
GATEWAY IDEAS 4. *Write in any gateway ideas you will use.*	Wrap-up		

Creating Opportunities
to Reach Junior Highers

OUR PRIMARY REASON FOR WORKING *with kids is to introduce them to a relationship with God. We are in the spirituality business. Foundational to our ministry with these kids is the realization that we exist to connect kids to a relationship with Jesus Christ . . . and if what we do with kids doesn't result in connecting kids to God, then we will inevitably be discouraged and frustrated with the results.*

—Mike Yaconelli
*1993 Youth Specialties
National Resource Seminar
for Youth Workers*

A COUPLE OF YEARS AGO, my wife, Carol, and I had the scare of our young parenting lives. I had just finished speaking at a family conference on the West Coast. With our three-year-old son, Mark (who models his life after Calvin in *Calvin and Hobbes*), we flew the friendly skies of United back into the busiest airport in the world, O'Hare Airport in Chicago. We exited the plane and looked for a cart to load the ten thousand toys we had taken on the flight to keep Mark occupied. After securing a cart, I turned around and asked Carol, "Where is Mark?" For the next thirty seconds we played the "I thought he was with you" parental game. Realizing he wasn't with either of us, I sprinted to the front of the airport terminal looking at each little kid that I passed to make sure it wasn't him. At the same time Carol ran into the United Service Center crying, "My son is lost." They took a quick description and sprang into action.

As they and we searched, my emotions ranged from hope to worry to sheer terror as I thought of the potential danger that my son could be in. After what seemed like an eternity, I looked down at the end of the terminal and saw the most moving sight of my life—two United flight attendants walking toward us, hand in hand with our son.

With tears in my eyes, thinking he was traumatized, I hugged Mark and asked him, "Are you okay?" He wasn't shook up at all. He thought the trip to the other end of the terminal was one of the greatest adventures of his young life . . . which was about to be shortened. As I walked out of the airport, now handcuffed to my son, I cannot describe the feelings that I experienced on the emotional roller coaster of nearly losing one of my kids. That experience parallels how I feel about reaching junior high students.

First, my son was lost . . . in danger . . . and didn't even know it. That describes well this generation of junior highers. Many have walked away, or been enticed away, from a relationship with God who loves them like a mother and a father. Many will suffer serious consequences of that separation. Yet they don't even know the dangerous state that they're in.

Secondly, I didn't find my own son. Someone else heard that our son was lost and dropped everything they were doing to bring our son back into the arms of his parents.

In our society, there is no group that is more open, more available, more needy, or more obviously headed down a road that could lead to severe consequences than junior high kids. We can turn these kids' lives around when we develop outreach ministries designed to attract junior high students to the Christian faith.

In this chapter, you'll get suggestions for outreach goals, game plan ideas for developing an effective outreach ministry to ready-to-visit junior high students, possible results you can hope to achieve, and "gateway" ideas to motivate casual junior high students to move on to a decision to follow Jesus.

POSSIBLE GOALS

Unchurched junior high students are open, available, and willing to come to events that are fun. Many junior high campuses are hurting due to budget cutbacks and are more than willing for you to volunteer to tutor, coach, or help in other practical ways. Junior high students in your church are willing to invite their friends to your group if they have confidence in the event.

As you select your goals, remember that reaching kids before high school is essential. Set bold goals and move forward. You may be surprised at the results. You can select your goals from the list below, or create your own that you feel will maximize the potential in your group.

• Have each of our kids select and regularly pray for one unchurched friend.

- Begin a monthly junior high outreach ministry that kids are excited to invite their friends to.
- Motivate our junior highers by letting them design the outreach events.
- Provide an outreach camp that will be attractive to unchurched kids.
- Provide opportunities for our junior high kids to receive training for evangelism.
- Pull off a junior high event that is wild enough to get talked about at school (without getting myself fired).
- Follow up each visitor to youth group with a letter and phone call within one week.
- Help junior highers clearly understand the claims of Jesus Christ.
- Give junior highers the opportunity to make a commitment to Jesus Christ.
- Develop the reputation of being a fun group.
- Give every new junior higher a warm welcome and an adult who is crazy about him or her.
- Invite every junior higher in our city to an outreach event.

GAME PLAN IDEAS

The following game plan ideas are designed to give your junior high ministry tools that your students can use to expose their friends positively to the Christian faith. They are divided into three categories: Relational, Conceptual, and Action ideas.

RELATIONAL IDEAS

"Come and See Me" Cards

A great way to reach out to students is to attend their ball games, recitals, performances, contests, shows, and other events in which your kids shine. Tell kids you want to watch them, and get all the information you need to schedule these visits by handing out "Come and See Me" cards. Use the back of the card to jot down pertinent information that comes up in conversation or to record names of other related student contacts.

Come and See Me

Fill this out when you would like to have me come watch you!

Your Name _____ Phone _____

Name of Event _____ Date _____

Location _____ Time _____

Kid-Friendly Environments

How many times have you been to an outreach event and the first thing that is communicated is the rules? This is followed by singing songs that no unchurched junior higher has ever heard of. The entire event begins with a negative start. No wonder unchurched kids are staying away in droves.

The atmosphere of your youth meetings may well be a determining factor in whether junior highers will invite their friends and whether these new kids will return. Use some of the following ideas to create an environment that new junior high kids will like and want to return to.

Have music playing when kids arrive. Junior highers like noise and action. Playing upbeat, familiar-sounding music as they arrive is a great way to set the new students at ease. They will feel at home and have the sense that this church experience might actually be fun.

Don't let kids come in until the meeting is ready to start. By doing this you create excitement and anticipation for the meeting. We had a group of kids take a roll of slide pictures every week. The following week, our students came into the youth room with music playing and slides of themselves flashing on the wall. Not only does this create a fun environment, but because kids love to see themselves in pictures, this attracted junior high kids into the room.

Build affirmation into your environment. To help kids feel comfortable and want to return, make sure all students are greeted, avoid inside jokes, provide lyrics for songs, and go out of your way to meet students and learn their names.

Doorknob Encouragement

For new or fringe junior highers, nothing beats letting them know they are noticed. A fun way to affirm your kids is to fill paper bags with candy, an affirming note, and some encouraging verses of Scripture. The outside of the bag is decorated with the name of the student and colorful designs. Simply cut a hole in the top of the bag that is just big enough to slip on a doorknob and you're finished. It can be waiting for them when they come home from school or when they get up in the morning.

Enhance Your Facility

Many youth rooms can resemble prison cells. Kids are sitting in the same chairs, facing the same direction, and looking at the same 1949 Holy Land map on the wall. Steve Dickie and Darrell Pearson, in their book, *Creative Programming Ideas for Junior High Ministry* (Youth Specialties, 1992), list several ways to create a kid-friendly atmosphere in your room.

1. Collect old pillows or seat cushions and throw them on the floor for kids to sit on.
2. Create a bulletin board filled with photos, flyers, and upcoming events announcements.
3. Create school banners with the names of your kids' schools on them, and hang them on the wall.
4. Decorate your room in a different theme each week.
5. Frequent auctions and garage sales. You can pick up all sorts of stuff to add to your youth room.
6. Gather old sofas, chairs, and other furniture to create a lounge area.
7. Hang banners, signs, or posters.
8. Have a soda machine in your room.
9. Have a video on screen as kids arrive.
10. Paint, wallpaper, or design graphics on the walls.
11. Provide snacks as the kids arrive (or as they leave).
12. Rearrange the chairs into a different formation each week.
13. Set up a table in your room stocked with flyers about your ministry.
14. Set up inexpensive board or table games throughout your room.
15. Take photos of your group. Enlarge them and hang them on the wall.
16. Using duct tape, create a four-square court on the floor.
17. Videotape the students as they arrive and play it back for them.

Get High School Students Involved

While speaking at a high school conference in Jackson, Mississippi, I met two remarkable high school students. That fall they had started co-leading a weekly on-campus outreach Bible study with a handful of junior high girls. Now, six months later, they had sixty junior high girls attending. They were planning a retreat and wanted advice on how to put one together.

In my own junior high ministry, spiritually mature high school juniors and seniors are some of the most effective volunteers. The kids like and respect them, and many already have relationships with unchurched kids. If you are looking for more help, and want to expand your outreach to junior high kids, high school students can be a great help.

Get on Campus

In my first couple of years in youth ministry, I coached everything from a seventh grade boys basketball team to a sixth grade girls kickball team. I was able to get time on campus, make friends with teachers and administrators, and had a ministry to kids I wouldn't have met otherwise.

Junior high teachers and administrators are swamped due to time demands, overcrowded classes, and budget cutbacks. Secular schools will not allow you to set up a soapbox and preach, but there are several ways to get on campus: coaching, tutoring, helping to run school events, etc. One youth worker in our town developed a ministry of picture taking. He took live action shots of the wrestling team each week, developed them, and brought them to school the next week. Whenever this guy walked on campus, he was mobbed. Most athletes love seeing themselves in action, and he was able to build great relationships with the students as a result.

One caution: When on a school campus, play by their rules. Make an appointment with the principal, find out what the rules are, and honor them. Many administrators have to deal with people who abuse the privilege of being on campus. Approaching campus access with a servant attitude will earn the trust of administrators and provide open doors.

Lifestyles of the Young and Degenerate

A great way to have fun with your junior highers and build attendance at your youth group is to take a video camera to your kids' houses when they are not home, and (with the parents' prior permission) videotape their bedroom in whatever shape you find it. Film the kids' rooms, pets, baby pictures, and so on. Interview each kid's mom or dad about the kid's "habits." Do your best Robin Leach impression, then announce on Sunday that the midweek program will feature *them*. (P.S.: Setting up your students can be a lot of fun. We set up guys with Barbie dolls under their pillows and "found" tons of candy bars under the girls' beds.)

A note of caution: Not all kids will appreciate this idea—particularly those struggling with feelings of poor self-esteem. Before using this idea, think ahead about how it could impact kids in your group.

Test Your Junior High Climate

A group of churches in the Northwest completed a recent church growth study of over sixty churches. They studied statistics for attendance, age, and income, and then surveyed the attitudes and thinking of the leaders. They discovered that "whether a church was stagnant or growing depended directly on the attitudes of the leaders." Where the church leaders were positive, flexible, confident, cheerful, and goal-oriented, the church was vibrant, alive, and growing. But where the leaders had little vision, creativity, or exciting goals, the church was stagnant and paralyzed.[1]

Junior highers can sense whether they are valued, accepted, and wanted. Not only is the atmosphere of your meetings and facilities important in attracting kids, but the climate of the church is equally essential. The following questionnaire (found on page 60) is not scientific by any means, but can give you some idea of how "kid friendly" your church is for junior high students. Have your adult volunteers (and yourself) complete this survey; then tabulate the results and determine your kid-friendly quotient.

What is Your "Kid-Friendly" Quotient?

Check one answer per question.

Adults in our church view the junior highers as:

_____	A total nuisance	10 points
_____	Little as possible	7 points
_____	The church of tomorrow	3 points
_____	People who can contribute now	0 points

A junior higher's primary gift is:

_____	The gift of chaos	10 points
_____	The gift of hair	7 points
_____	The gift of idealism	3 points
_____	The gift of never saying, "We've never done it that way before"	0 points

The last time your junior highers were involved in your Sunday morning service was:

_____	The night the church burned down after the youth candlelight service	10 points
_____	When a kid fell into the baptismal	7 points
_____	Once last year	3 points
_____	In the last two months	0 points

When was the last time you allowed the junior highers to plan an event?

_____	You've got to be kidding	10 points
_____	Before I got fired at my last church	7 points
_____	Just before our last janitor quit	3 points
_____	In the last month	0 points

What task do you allow junior highers to do?

_____	Anything invisible to the world	10 points
_____	Anything visible, but unimportant	7 points
_____	Anything not requiring three years of church history	3 points
_____	Anything they have the resources to accomplish	0 points

When you give junior highers something to do, you:

_____	Tell them in detail how to do it	10 points
_____	Give them specific guidelines	5 points
_____	Give them considerable freedom	0 points

How often do you go behind junior highers' backs and "check up" on them?

_____	All of the time	10 points
_____	Most of the time	7 points
_____	Some of the time	3 points
_____	Never	0 points

How do you spend the majority of your time?

_____	Dealing with program & problems	10 points
_____	With a computer or Ideas book	7 points
_____	With your therapist	3 points
_____	With junior high students	0 points

Do you ever say, "I'll just do it myself; it will be easier"?

_____	Yes	10 points
_____	No	0 points

Are you reluctant to ask junior highers to help with the program?

_____	Yes	10 points
_____	No	0 points

TOTAL POINTS _____

The scoring system is as follows:

0-30   Junior highers will flourish in your group.

31-60   Junior highers will feel appreciated in your group and there is good opportunity for growth.

61-90   You may be struggling to enable kids to feel wanted, significant, and valuable. You may want to do some more groundwork.

91-100   It may be time to TP the senior pastor's house and look for an easier career, like selling air conditioners to Siberians.

The results of this survey can lead to a great discussion regarding how to make your church friendly to new junior high students.

Thirty Great Things You Can Do with a Kid

The ministry of Jesus Christ demonstrates the value of spending time with people in their world. Junior highers are available and usually more than willing to let you hang out with them. Most of the following ideas are great for building relationships with students you hope will begin to feel a part of your group.

1. All-night Monopoly/Pictionary/Trivial Pursuit (Note: All-night events work better with people of the same sex).
2. Ask a junior higher to teach you how to use your computer.
3. Build a model.
4. Sit down over a Coke.
5. Do a photo essay of other kids' rooms/or the kid's own room.
6. Go bowling.
7. Go rock climbing/hiking/cross-country skiing.
8. Go skating.
9. Go to a school event (there's always something going on), preferably not just a popular activity. If you show up at the oboe recital, you WILL be noticed!
10. Go to a movie or rent a video.
11. Go to a professional/college sporting event.
12. Go to the mall.
13. Have a junior higher teach you how to program your VCR.
14. Have a Nintendo overnighter.
15. Have devotions together (read Bible and pray together).
16. Make a birthday cake for one of the other kids in the youth group.
17. Make a video.
18. Practice your Boy Scout knots.
19. Ride bikes.
20. Ride zeppelins.
21. Stay up all night and watch a meteor shower together (the best showers are after midnight).
22. Throw a Frisbee.
23. Throw a party.
24. Tutor the kid in a subject he or she is struggling with.
25. Have the junior higher tutor you in a subject you are struggling with.

26. Wash a car together (preferably yours; maybe the kid's bike).

27. Work on a mural for the youth room.

28. Work through a Bible study book together.

29. Work together on a building project for Habitat for Humanity or a similar one day/one afternoon service project.

30. Write a song together.

CONCEPTUAL IDEAS

The following ideas are designed to help junior highers better understand the Christian faith.

Student Testimonies

Kids listen to kids. I once spoke at an event in Canada called Youth Quake. What an intimidating event! It is Canada's largest youth event; four thousand teenagers, the Canadian Women's Olympic Volleyball Team, big-name bands, etc. During the middle of one of the meetings, a very nervous teenager stepped up to the microphone to talk about his faith in Christ. As he struggled (and he did struggle) to speak, you could have heard a pin drop. Four thousand students were riveted as he described the impact that Christ had in his life. When he finished, he was greeted with a thunderous standing ovation. It left the rest of us who were speaking wishing that we were teenagers. Kids listen best to other kids, and outreach meetings of four to four thousand are a great place to have your junior highers talk about what their relationship with Christ means to them.

Christmas I.Q. Test

Christmas is a great time to gather a crowd of junior highers, and taking the following test (on pages 63 and 64) is a wonderful way to communicate the real meaning of Christmas. Have them work on the test in groups, give prizes to the group with the most correct answers, and wrap up by having people explain what the coming of Christ means to them.

CHRISTMAS I.Q. TEST

1. As long as Christmas has been celebrated, it has been on December 25th.
   ☐ True ☐ False

2. Joseph was from
   a. Bethlehem d. Egypt
   b. Jerusalem e. Minnesota
   c. Nazareth   f. none of the above

3. How did Mary and Joseph travel to Bethlehem?
   a. camel   c. walked
   b. donkey   d. Volkswagen
      e. Joseph walked; Mary rode a donkey
      f. Who knows?

4. Mary and Joseph were married when Mary became pregnant.
   ☐ True ☐ False

5. Mary and Joseph were married when Jesus was born.
   ☐ True ☐ False

6. Mary was a virgin when she delivered Jesus.
   ☐ True ☐ False

7. What did the innkeeper tell Mary and Joseph?
   a. "There is no room at the inn."
   b. "I have a stable you can use."
   c. "Come back after the Christmas rush and I should have some vacancies."
   d. both a and b
   e. What innkeeper?

8. Jesus was delivered in a
   a. stable   d. barn
   b. hospital e. unknown
   c. cave

9. A manger is a
   a. stable for domestic animals
   b. wooden hay storage bin
   c. feeding trough
   d. barn
   e. supervisor of a Dairy Queen in Mobile, Alabama

10. Which animals does the Bible say were present at Jesus' birth?
    a. cows, sheep, goats
    b. cows, donkeys, sheep
    c. sheep and goats only
    d. miscellaneous barnyard animals
    e. lions, tigers, bears (oh my!)
    f. none of the above

11. Who saw the "star in the East"?
    a. shepherds
    b. Mary and Joseph
    c. some kings
    d. both a and c
    e. none of the above

12. How many angels spoke to the shepherds?
    a. one
    b. three
    c. a multitude
    d. none of the above

13. What sign did the angel tell the shepherds to look for?
    a. This Way to Jesus
    b. a star over Bethlehem
    c. a baby that doesn't cry
    d. a house with a Christmas tree
    e. a baby in a stable
    f. none of the above

14. What did the angels sing?
    a. "Joy to the World, the Lord Is Come"
    b. "Alleluia"
    c. "Unto us a child is born, unto us a son is given"
    d. "Glory to God in the highest . . ."
    e. "Glory to the Newborn King"
    f. "My Sweet Lord"

15. What is a heavenly host?
    a. the angel at the gate of heaven
    b. the angel who invites people to heaven
    c. the angel who serves drinks in heaven
    d. an angel choir
    e. an angel army
    f. none of the above

16. There was snow that first Christmas:
    a. only in Bethlehem
    b. all over Israel
    c. probably nowhere in Israel
    d. probably somewhere in Israel
    e. Mary and Joseph only dreamed of a white Christmas

17. The baby Jesus cried:
    a. when the doctor slapped Him on His behind
    b. when the little drummer boy started banging on his drum
    c. just like other babies cry
    d. He never cried

18. What is frankincense?
    a. a precious metal
    b. a precious fabric
    c. a precious perfume
    d. an Eastern monster story

19. What is myrrh?
    a. an easily-shaped metal
    b. a spice used for burying people
    c. a drink
    d. after-shave lotion
    e. none of the above

20. How many wise men came to see Jesus? _____
    (Write in the correct number.)

21. What does wise men or magi refer to?
    a. men of the educated class
    b. Eastern kings
    c. astrologers
    d. people smart enough to follow the star
    e. sages

22. The wise men found Jesus in a
    a. manger
    b. stable
    c. house
    d. Holiday Inn
    e. good mood

23. The wise men stopped in Jerusalem
    a. to inform Herod about Jesus
    b. to find out where Jesus was
    c. to ask about the star that they saw
    d. to get gas
    e. to buy presents for Jesus

24. Where do we find the Christmas story?
    a. Matthew
    b. Mark
    c. Luke
    d. John
    e. all of the above
    f. only a and b
    g. only a and c
    h. only a, b, and c
    i. only x, y, and z
    j. Aesop's Fables

25. When Joseph and Mary found out that Mary was pregnant with Jesus, what happened?
    a. they got married
    b. Joseph wanted to break the engagement
    c. Mary left town for three months
    d. an angel told them to go to Bethlehem
    e. both a and d
    f. both b and c

26. Who told Mary and Joseph to go to Bethlehem?
    a. an angel
    b. Mary's mother
    c. Herod
    d. Caesar Augustus
    e. Alexander the Great
    f. no one

27. Joseph took the baby Jesus to Egypt
    a. to show Him the pyramids
    b. to teach Him the wisdom of the Pharaohs
    c. to put Him in a basket in the reeds by the river
    d. to fulfill a dream he had
    e. to be taxed
    f. none of the above

28. I think that this test was
    a. super
    b. great
    c. fantastic
    d. all of the above

Answers to Christmas I.Q. Test

1. False. Not until the fourth century did it settle on the 25th. Other dates were accepted before then.
2. a. See Luke 2:3, 4.
3. f. The Bible doesn't say.
4. False. See Matthew 1:18.
5. False. See Luke 2:5.
6. True. See Matthew 1:25.
7. e. No word about the innkeeper. See Luke 2:7.
8. e. No word about it. See Luke 2:7.
9. c.
10. f. The Bible doesn't specify.
11. e. The wise men did (they were not kings). See Matthew 2:2.
12. a. See Luke 2:9.
13. f. See Luke 2:12. This verse mentions a manger, not (answer e) a stable.
14. d. See Luke 2:14.
15. e. Definition is an "army." (See Living Bible also.)
16. d. Mt. Hermon is sometimes snow covered.
17. c. We have no reason to believe He wouldn't cry.
18. c. By definition.
19. b. See John 19:39 or a dictionary.
20. No one knows. See Matthew 2:1.
21. c. See most any commentary. They were astrologers or "star gazers."
22. c. See Matthew 2:11.
23. b. See Matthew 2:1-2.
24. g. Mark begins with John the Baptist, John with "the Word."
25. f. See Matthew 1:19; Luke 1:39, 56.
26. d. See Luke 2:1, 4.
27. d. See Matthew 2:13.
28. d. Of course.

Tackle Tough Topics Creatively

Most junior high meetings include some kind of content wrap-up. If you have the gift of speaking but your kids don't have the gift of listening, you may want to try tackling tough topics.

When your content touches on felt needs of junior highers (things they are feeling or involved with), they will be much more inclined to give you a listen. A good example is the topic of fear. In my first junior high group, we sponsored a junior high "Fright Nite." We took the junior highers to a nearby park in the mountains and, after it got good and dark, began our meeting with singing. I interrupted the singing with a somber announcement that the ranger had just informed me that we would have to leave. An escaped convict, in prison for murder, had just escaped and was reported to be in our area. Just as the students started buying this story, one of our volunteers jumped out from behind a rock with a bloodcurdling scream. Kids went crazy. When they realized that the whole thing was a setup and began to pay attention, I said, "Tonight's wrap-up is about something we all have to learn to deal with: fear."

Their attention level and response to the content was the highest I had ever seen it. Unchurched kids are not interested in learning the names of the disciples, but they do have questions about tough issues. You may want to try tackling some of the following topics:

- Dating and relating
- Dealing with divorcing parents
- Does God really exist?
- How to build great friendships
- How to get better grades
- How to raise your parents
- How to make great decisions
- How to get up when you are down
- How to know if you are in love
- Is the Bible really true?
- Overcoming fear
- Overcoming insecurity
- Taking on temptation
- 25 ways to make money this summer
- Understanding the opposite sex

Take Junior Highers to Major Christian Events

Whether it's a major denominational event, a Christian concert, Gospel night at a theme park, or a week at your local Christian camp, taking junior highers on outreach trips may get a hearing that they wouldn't allow otherwise.

We took our junior highers to an annual weekend event called "The Road to Greatness." The event was organized by local youth workers who usually brought in an outstanding guest speaker. In a new setting, even the new students listened attentively and often responded to the message.

(P.S.: A fun addition to the weekend is to stay in a hotel. Our junior highers loved it. It was fun and they felt like adults. You can usually house four persons per room to keep the expenses down.)

Try the Unexpected

At my first junior high ministry we had a total of two junior high kids in the church—on a good Sunday. Feeling the need to grow to greater numbers (like four), we planned a series of four weekly outreach breakfasts leading up to what we hoped would be the big Christmas breakfast. After three weeks of promotion, fifteen showed up at our breakfast. We thought revival had broken out. At the end of the breakfast, Greg, one of our volunteers, came racing through the fellowship hall on his motorcycle. The noise was deafening and kids almost fell off their chairs. That day at school, we were the talk of the campus. Our church became known as the Church of the Holy Motorcycle.

The two subsequent weeks brought even bigger numbers as each week Greg raced through the breakfast. By the fourth (Christmas celebration) breakfast, we crammed in over one hundred kids. That morning, as the motorcycle raced through, all of the junior highers picked up their pieces of french toast and threw them "Frisbee style" at Greg. It took hours to clean the french toast off the walls, but it was worth it. Unchurched kids, many for the first time, were hearing about Jesus. Several students from that ministry met Christ and continue to walk with Him.

Many unchurched kids are convinced that the church, and God, are uptight, dull, negative, and boring. When we take a few risks, do the outrageous, and have fun, it blows their stereotypes of church and creates an openness to listen to the Gospel.

Use Video and Movies

Movies are the language of the American adolescent. Outstanding video resources are available that communicate the Christian faith to unchurched junior high kids, including:

Edge TV, (1-800-366-7788). High-quality, short topics, and comes with a leaders guide.

Selling Addiction/Consumer Seduction (Center for Media and Values, 1-310-202-1936). An outstanding, two-part video series that helps kids think critically about the alcohol and tobacco industries.

Sex, Lies & the Truth (Focus on the Family, 1-800-932-9123). A hard-hitting video about the consequences of sexual choices.

But Is It Safe? by Miles McPherson (Project Intercept, 4688 Alvarado Canyon Rd. Suite L, San Diego, CA 92120, 1-619-286-2501). Filmed on location at Chula Vista High School, Miles does a great job of speaking to churched and unchurched students at the same time.

God Loves Me, So What! (Family Films/Concordia, 1-800-325-2004). Featuring Guy Doud, this creative video series (3 videos, 20 min. each) examines choices. Funny and fast moving. Includes leader's guide, participant's flyers, etc.

Another way to communicate to junior high kids is to allow them to watch and discuss popular movies. A great resource for this is Dave Veerman's *Video Movies Worth Watching* (Baker Book House, 1992). He covers seventy-five popular movies, evaluates each film's quality, and supplies discussion questions and Bible references for further study.

What, Me a Christian?

The quiz *What Is a Christian?* on page 69 will enable your junior highers to think through some of their own assumptions as well as questions frequently raised by others. This quiz is not designed to provide answers (some of the questions may have no "correct" answer), but rather to make junior highers think about their own relationship with Christ. Give each person a copy of this true/false quiz and ask kids to circle T or F beside each statement. Then discuss the answers.

Helpful wrap-up Bible passages are John 3:1-16, Romans 8:28-38, and Ephesians 2:8-10.

WHAT IS A CHRISTIAN?

T F 1. The only thing one must do to be a Christian is to attend church on Sunday.

T F 2. The only thing one must do to be a Christian is to be a member of a church.

T F 3. A person becomes a Christian when he is baptized.

T F 4. A person becomes a Christian when she is confirmed.

T F 5. In order to be a Christian, you only have to believe that Jesus Christ died for your sins.

T F 6. All real Christians are "born again" Christians.

T F 7. Every member of this church is a Christian.

T F 8. Jesus was a Christian.

T F 9. Only those people who belong to the _____ Church are Christians.

T F 10. Most people in my church only say they are Christians, but they really are not Christians.

T F 11. To be a Christian one must read the Bible regularly.

T F 12. Everyone who goes to church is a Christian.

T F 13. All Christians believe the same things.

T F 14. Being a Christian means that I can't do all the fun things that my friends do.

T F 15. One can be a Christian and still believe that drinking alcohol is okay.

T F 16. Once one is a Christian, she never sins again.

T F 17. You can tell that a person is a Christian by the way he acts.

T F 18. Christians do not swear or curse.

T F 19. Christians love everyone.

T F 20. My parents are Christians.

T F 21. As a Christian, I must do the right things in order for God to continue to love me.

T F 22. God loves Christians more than He loves non-Christians.

T F 23. God does not allow Christians to get hurt.

T F 24. Most of my friends are Christians.

T F 25. I am a Christian.

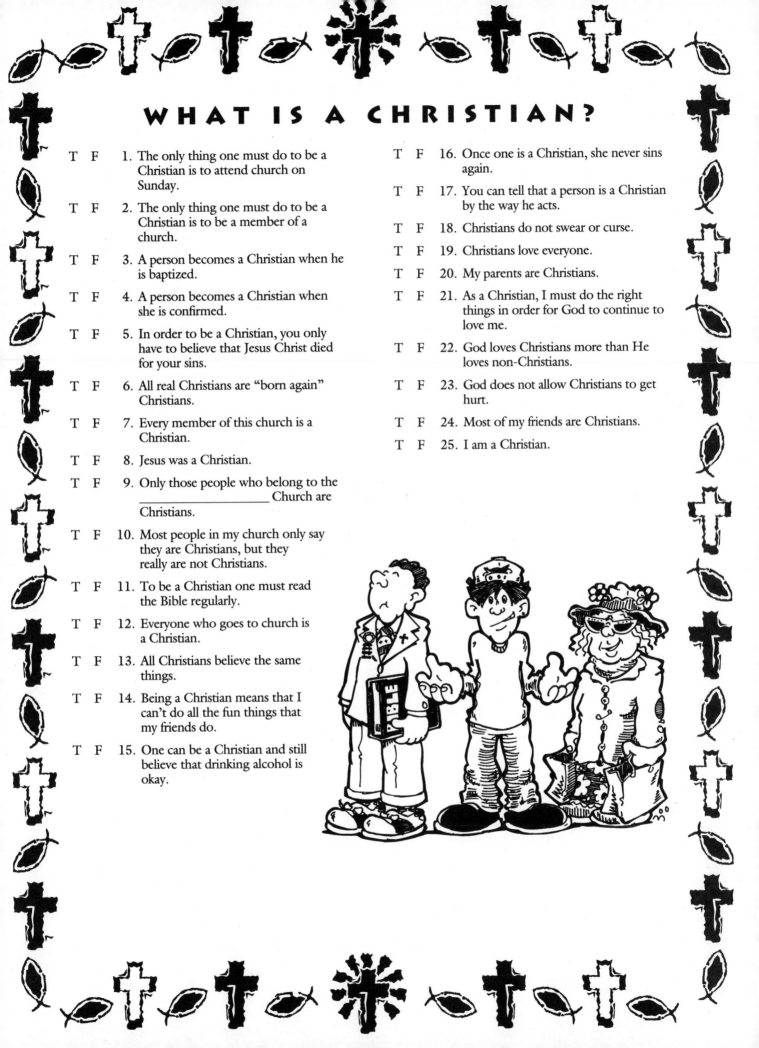

C H A P T E R   S I X

ACTION IDEAS

Drive-In Theater

Youth worker Randy Phillips in Bellevue, Washington, and his kids turn their fellowship hall into a drive-in theater for one week each year. The preparation is amazing. The kids make special ramps to safely drive in and park cars they have borrowed. Van and car seats are set up and a large screen is installed. They set up a snack bar and decorate the room to look like a fifties drive-in theater. They show movies like *Back to the Future,* and junior highers flock into the church, many for the first time. The key to this event is student involvement in the planning, construction, and setup of the event. The more involvement the students have, the more excited they will be about bringing their friends.

Junior Higher Scavenger Hunt

This scavenger hunt can dramatically increase the attendance of your youth group in one evening. Divide into groups of four, each group having an adult driver and car. Give groups forty-five minutes to find, and bring back to the youth group, as many junior high students as possible. Create a long list with points for different types of kids. Ideas for the scavenger hunt can include the following:

- Sixth-grade boy—100 points
- Sixth-grade girl—100 points
- Seventh-grade boy with freckles—150 points
- Seventh-grade girl with braces—200 points
- A student wearing pajamas—200 points
- Eighth-grade class president—250 points
- Eighth-grade girl—200 points
- A couple that are dating each other—300 points
- Junior high twins—500 points
- Junior higher who can juggle—500 points (must demonstrate)
- A junior higher who has never been to the group—750 points

Add as many other categories as you want. The kids will bring lots of their friends back, and you can wrap up the meeting with a skit, brief message, and information about your next meeting.

Kidnap Events

Hold an event crazy enough not to have been imagined and well planned enough not to have been expected. A committee of kids must

70

telephone parents and prearrange the kidnap of their young people. Then, on the set date, the kids are kidnapped by the committee and taken somewhere for a special get-together. Complete surprise is essential. Good results have been had with a "Kidnap Breakfast" (six a.m. menu of pizza, soft drinks, and watermelon) and a "Kidnap All-Night Film Festival" and lock-in at the church.

Operation Andrew

Operation Andrew is a great way to increase attendance at your outreach events by helping your junior highers catch a vision for bringing their friends. Begin by doing a short study with your key kids regarding Andrew, who was consistently bringing people to Jesus.

Andrew bringing Simon (John 1:40-42)

Andrew bringing the boy with loaves and fish (John 6:8, 9)

Andrew bringing the Greeks (John 12:20-22)

Wrap up the study by having the students fill out a copy of the Operation Andrew Card (page 72) and keep the card in their Bibles. This card works best when used with a specific outreach event like a camp, ski trip, or musical concert.

Operation Andrew

Bringing my friends to Jesus Christ

John 1:40-42   John 6:8, 9   John 12:20-22

List below the friends you would like to invite.

_____

_____

_____

_____

_____

_____

Pizza Bash

My most successful outreach event, the Pizza Bash, combines food, fun, and action in a single evening. We planned and promoted the event during the first three weeks of school. We printed business cards like this:

We included the location, date, and time, and students passed them out to their friends. Kids arrived early to music playing and could jump in on volleyball, basketball, and Ping-Pong games. Each student filled out a registration card, which could also be used as an entry for a door prize. That gave us our follow-up list. Kids ate until they were full, then watched skits, followed by three students sharing their testimonies. After we drew for the door prize, the evening ended with a slide show of our group in action (camps, etc.), followed by passing out a calendar of our events to each student and inviting them back the next week.

Pre-Event Activities

With junior high outreach events, it is important to realize that the meeting starts not at the scheduled time, but when the kids arrive. This time is called the "pre-event" time and will either be a bore or a blast. Some of the following ideas will help you get started on the right foot.

- *Pyramids.* Ask a group if they can build a three-person pyramid. Then find a group that can build a six-person pyramid. Try for 10, 16, 21 . . . an all-female pyramid . . . all eighth graders . . . whatever you can think of.

- *Flamingos.* Same idea as pyramids, but try to get a group of six to stand on the fewest number of legs possible; they can get on each other's backs or whatever it takes to have the least number of body parts touching the ground.

- *Dares.*
    —Three people standing on their heads and whistling.
    —Wheelbarrow race down the aisles.
    —Arranging themselves in rows by age, grades, or birthdays.
    —A group that starts humming the "Leave It to Beaver" theme until everyone in the room joins in.
- *Polls.* Have students go around the room conducting various polls:
    —The names of twenty TV characters seen on Thursday nights.
    —The names of ten bald people.
    —The brands or styles or colors of underwear being worn in the room.
    —Favorite cartoon characters.
    —Favorite and worst TV shows and commercials.
    —Average shoe size (male and female).
    —The fingers folks use to pick their noses.
    —The most photos carried in one wallet.
- *Graffiti wall.* Where kids can write, draw, and paint whatever they want.
- *Trivia.* Before the program begins, have one person call out trivia questions, asking those who know the answers to make a strange noise. The first one to make a strange noise gets to answer. If the answer is correct, you give him a silly gift (a candy bar, for example). Play until you run out of prizes or you have to start the program.
- *Shake hands.* Give two people a dollar, secretly. These two people are instructed to shake hands and exchange names with the rest of the group. However, when these two meet their tenth person (tell them to keep count), they should scream as loud as they can and give that person the dollar.
- *Pastor's office shuffle.* Take a group of students into the pastor's office and see how quickly they can rearrange his or her library books. (This antic works best during your last week on the job.)

Ski Retreat

I hate skiing for one reason—I am the worst skier that ever hit the slopes (which I did often). But each winter, I took junior highers skiing for one reason—they were more comfortable inviting their unchurched friends to a ski retreat than to a church camp. The weekend was filled with skiing, skits, great food, no sleep, and the best youth speaker we could find.

The key isn't skiing per se, but finding out what junior highers in your area love to do, then wrapping an outreach event around that activity. The best way to discover this is to ask your kids. For us, their answer was skiing . . . unfortunately.

Student-planned Outreach Events

Giving junior highers the opportunity to plan outreach programs gives them ownership and confidence. They will be more likely to bring their friends to events that they have planned.

The Youth Group Planning Survey found on page 76 will enable your students to plan the major areas for your outreach ministry. Letting them brainstorm the topics, recreation, and outreach activities will motivate them to invite their friends with increased confidence.

YOUTH GROUP PLANNING SURVEY

TOPICS

Circle 10 topics that your friends would be interested in.

1. Friendships
2. Dating
3. How to overcome discouragement
4. How to handle my parents' divorce
5. Evolution vs. Creation
6. Tackling temptation
7. Handling anger
8. Death
9. Drugs
10. Ecology
11. Faith
12. Getting along with brothers and sisters
13. Getting along with parents
14. Getting along with friends
15. Getting along with adults
16. God's will
17. Group pressure
18. Hunger
19. Identity
20. Independence
21. Jealousy
22. Love
23. Sex

Your Ideas:

24. _____
    _____
25. _____
    _____
26. _____
    _____

METHODS

Circle 4 methods that you most enjoy.

1. Skits
2. Object lessons
3. Student speakers
4. Discussion
5. Panel of adults
6. Panel of high schoolers
7. Movies
8. Videos
9. Roleplaying
10. Speaker
11. Group study
12. Workbooks

Your ideas:

13. _____
14. _____
15. _____

RECREATION

Circle 8 activities you'd be most excited about inviting friends to.

1. Beach trip
2. Snow skiing
3. Waterskiing
4. Softball
5. Volleyball
6. Baseball
7. Football night
8. Bike hike
9. Swimming
10. Progressive dinner
11. Pizza party
12. Horseback riding
13. Miniature golf
14. Tubing
15. Go-carts
16. Bowling
17. Trampolines
18. Roller-skating
19. Ice-skating
20. Dance
21. Cookout
22. Canoeing
23. Air hockey tournament

Your Ideas:

24. _____
    _____
25. _____
    _____
26. _____
    _____

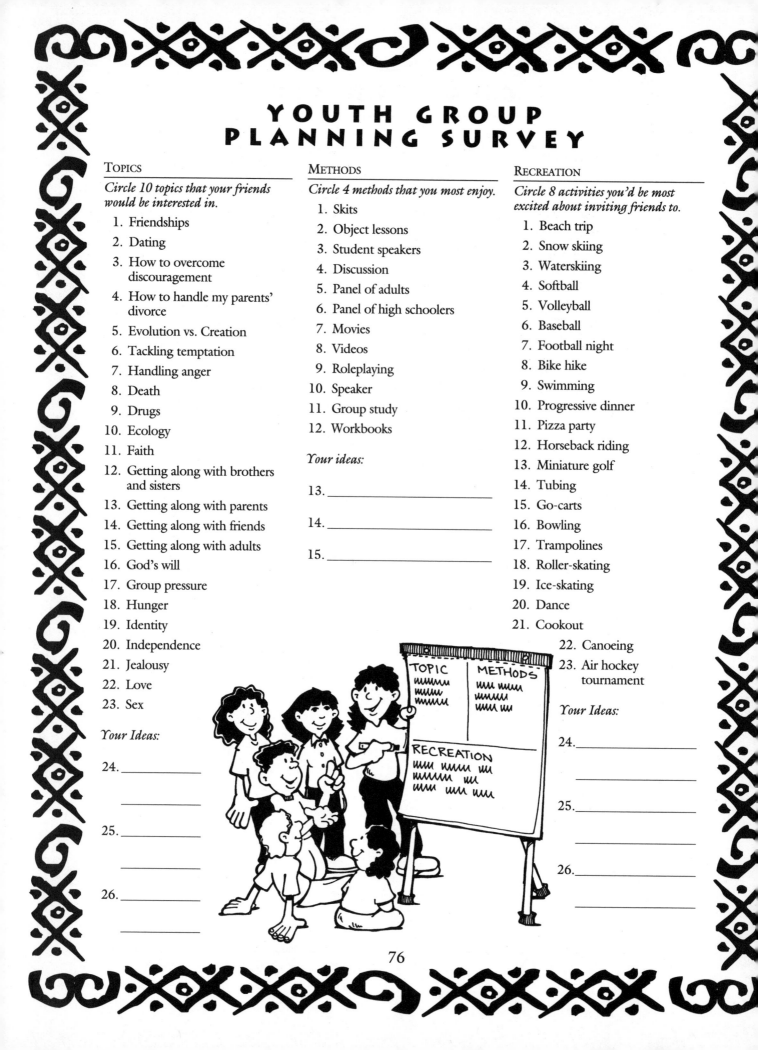

CHAPTER SIX

WHAT YOU HOPE TO ACHIEVE

In their book *Reaching Youth Today* (Judson Press, 1983), Hargrove and Jones are right when they say that faith in Jesus Christ can equip a teen with "a sense of purpose which appeals to the idealistic, providing a strong sense of identity and self-worth." A solid outreach ministry will help junior highers discover that in Christ they are accepted, loved, and back in the arms of their heavenly Father.

Some of the gains you can anticipate and pray for include:

You will be on the cutting edge of youth ministry. It is imperative that the church in America begin to reach kids at a younger age. When you intentionally develop outreach ministries to junior high youth, you are on the front lines of where the church needs to be.

Junior high outreach programs will give your students evangelism tools they can use. Many junior highers would like to share the Gospel with their friends. Many who are uncomfortable verbally sharing their faith will willingly invite their friends to a good outreach event. This allows the majority of your students to use these "tools" with their friends.

Junior highers will develop confidence in the Gospel. As your students see their friends becoming Christians, their confidence that the Gospel is good news begins to grow. Students will be amazed that their friends are receptive, and later that amazement will grow into confidence.

Your junior high ministry will grow. Outreach ministries attract new students. Sometimes the growth is gradual, occasionally, dramatic. Excitement builds as students see increasing numbers at their events.

Outreach programs give your students a meaningful chance to contribute to the ministry. Your students are not just attending the event, they are praying and seeking to bring their friends. This creates purpose and excitement for your kids. One of my favorite ministry moments is having junior high students introduce friends they have brought to an event. They are so excited that their friends are there and can't wait to introduce them.

Your overall church attendance will grow. Many parents of junior highers live in fear of the unhealthy things their teenager could get involved in. In the last few years, I have noticed parents going to whatever church their teenager likes, just to make sure their child has good role models in his or her life. A good outreach ministry will help your church become the "place to be" in your community. Developing a good junior high outreach ministry may be the single most explosive church growth tool.

Junior high students will enter into a relationship with God. My primary reason for working with kids is to introduce them to a relationship with God. Whether students raise their hands, walk forward, sign a commitment card, or talk to me personally, there is no greater thrill than introducing junior highers to Jesus Christ. With their whole life ahead of them, they now have the opportunity to walk that path hand in hand with their Lord and Savior.

GATEWAYS: LEADING JUNIOR HIGHERS ON TO SPIRITUAL GROWTH

Know the Purpose of Your Meetings

Willow Creek Community Church in Barrington, Illinois, has grown from zero to over fifteen thousand in the last twenty years. While there are many reasons for their growth, their effectiveness in moving new believers from visiting to being ready to grow is one of the keys. The reason for this is their clear-cut plan. The purpose of their Sunday morning services is outreach; almost every week, they issue an invitation to those wanting to know more or grow further to attend their Wednesday evening "New Community" services. Some of your casual students may be ready for a further step if you can offer them opportunities for further, more in-depth involvement.

Camp Follow-up Nights

Many of our junior highers' first events were camps or retreats. The key was to turn that first experience into weekly attendance. Each year, we followed up our ski weekend with a ski retreat reunion two weeks later. We showed videos of the retreat, had students share regarding decisions they had made, showed clips of ski movies, and invited the speaker back for a follow-up talk. Most of the new students returned and discovered that the weekly meetings could be fun and exciting.

Combine Outreach and Spiritual Growth

Getting a junior high kid to a fun outreach event is usually easier than getting him back for "church." Kids who knew the ski trip would be great weren't as sure about the Bible study the following Wednesday night. Combining events with *both* outreach and spiritual growth components attracts the students and nurtures their faith. Almost any combination will work well: basketball tournaments with a six-week series on dating and relating; a twenty-foot-long banana split with a talk on tackling temptation, a tractor pull and Bible study—almost any combination will do. The key is combining a spiritual growth experience with something the junior high students don't want to miss.

Hold Events That Are Longer in Length

This is probably the single most effective way to develop commitment and foster interest in spiritual growth. Whether it's a camp, retreat, wilderness trip, or ski weekend, the event should encompass fun, good content, relationship building, and a bona fide opportunity for kids to both meet Christ and start on the path to discipleship.

Invest in Kids' Parents

Parents of kids from unchurched homes may be nervous about their kids' growing involvement in the church. For some, having their kid get involved in the church can be intimidating. It conjures up images of their son or daughter giving away all of their possessions, dropping out of school, shaving their head, and selling pencils at the airport. They may wonder if this will mean even less time with their child, and whether your church can be trusted.

Trust is usually earned instead of given. Several ways you can build trust with the parents are as follows:

Keep them informed. Send flyers, brochures, and any material that you have that presents your church positively (and doesn't ask for money).

Get them involved. A Back-to-School Nite or a Parent-Teen Relay Nite can demonstrate to the parents that the group is fun, wholesome, and a positive influence on their junior higher. A great idea for a fun night is a "Closet Raid," where the kids and parents raid each others' closets and come dressed to the meeting like each other. The fun can continue with skits and roleplays where they reverse roles and interact in typical "family" situations.

Build a relationship. Shortly after I became a Christian and began attending church, my parents (fun, executive-type, unchurched people) had some reservations. Some of the volunteer staff guys from the church stopped by one day just to say hello. My parents loved them. They were bright, articulate, and none wore robes and sandals. One visit set my folks at ease and opened the door to further involvement in the church. Sometimes by just meeting with a parent, you can set him or her at ease and enable students to move on to spiritual growth with their parents' support.

The following ten ideas are also great ways to win the trust of parents:

1. Visit each parent in their home
2. Have a parents information meeting
3. Set up a Parents Advisory Council
4. Send a monthly newsletter to all the parents
5. Conduct a seminar for parents
6. Plan annual family camps and retreats
7. Help your kids to develop appreciation for their parents
8. Have your kids put on a Parents Appreciation Banquet
9. Have a Parents Panel at a youth group meeting
10. Develop a parents resource library

Personal Invitation

The closer you are to students, the greater your potential for walking them across the bridge into a growing relationship with Christ. Time spent with kids between meetings can be more important than the meetings themselves for moving students to new spiritual levels.

Endnotes

1. Gary Inrig, *Hearts of Iron, Feet of Clay* (Chicago: Moody Press, 1979), 55-56.

Creating Spiritual Growth Opportunities for Junior Highers

D R. ROBERT LAURENT, IN HIS BOOK *Keeping Your Teen in Touch with God,* states that over 50 percent of Christian teenagers will sit in church next Sunday morning; yet within two years, only 30 percent of these kids will still be around. George Gallup reports that 40 percent of all teenagers believe in astrology, 30 percent read astrology columns daily, and 93 percent know their astrological sign. Gallup further reveals that 65 percent of evangelical teens never read their Bibles and thirty-three percent feel that religion is out of date and out of touch.[1]

Taking junior high spiritual growth seriously means giving kids opportunities to develop and use their faith. This requires patience, faith, and all of the creativity you can muster. In this chapter, you'll receive principles and ideas for setting goals, anticipating gains, and developing your game plan for junior high spiritual growth. You'll also receive suggestions for gateway ideas to help junior highers move into a lifestyle of service.

POSSIBLE GOALS

Establishing spiritual growth goals for your junior highers will take into account both the needs of the whole group and the potential of the students who are ready to move faster spiritually. Ask yourself four questions prior to setting goals for junior high spiritual growth:

1. What spiritual growth needs does my *whole group* have?
2. If I knew that I couldn't fail, what would I like to accomplish spiritually with the *whole group?*
3. Which students within the group are "softhearted" and ready to run at a faster clip spiritually?
4. If I knew that I couldn't fail, what would I like to accomplish with my "softhearted" students?

You may find the following goals helpful in encouraging students to grow spiritually:

- Give each junior higher a consistent relationship with a volunteer who is praying for him or her.
- Give each junior higher a positive relationship with an encouraging adult in your church.
- Give each junior higher an understanding of the basics of the Christian faith.
- Give each junior higher the opportunity to contribute to an aspect of your morning worship service.
- Give each of your students the opportunity to participate in a small group Bible study.
- Help your students to identify and act on changes that need to occur in their lives.
- Help your students to learn to pray together.
- Place junior highers in several different kinds of worship experiences.
- Put junior highers in an environment where they have to learn to depend on God.
- Teach each student to study the Bible.

GAME PLAN IDEAS

RELATIONAL IDEAS

Accountability Relationships

Major events like camps and retreats can bring about life-changing decisions. I have found it helpful to develop accountability relationships after these events to help the junior highers stick to some of the decisions they have made.

This also works well in other areas. For example, a young person is having difficulty getting his homework done. We can meet with him or her each week to help them map out their study plan, or invite them over to our house for a weekly "study hall." Arrangements like this work best when the student wants to do it. Make kids aware of accountability relationships and then let them suggest specific options to you.

Body Balloon Burst

Everyone in the room is part of the body. Those whose last names begin with A-G are a foot; H-N, a hand; O-S, a mouth; and T-Z, a rear end.

When the leader calls "Go!" the kids form complete bodies of six people each—two hands, two feet, one mouth, and one rear end. Once a body is complete, the two feet carry one of the hands up to the leader and receive a balloon. Only the hand can carry the balloon. The two hands then hold the balloon while the mouth blows it up. Once the balloon is blown up, the rear end sits on it. The first body to pop its balloon is the winner.

This game graphically illustrates that a body is made up of many parts, each with a different contribution to make. After the game is over, read I Corinthians 12:12-26, and briefly discuss how the cooperation (or lack thereof) they experienced in the game relates to Paul's teaching on the body of Christ.

Compliment Contest

The average junior high student is better at chopping someone down than building him up. If some of your kids have trouble saying nice things to each other, try this. Seat the group in a circle around one person who is seated in a chair in the middle of the circle. The person in the middle chooses one person that she will compliment, then the person to that student's right will try to beat her compliment with a better compliment. After hearing both compliments, the person who is the object of the compliments decides which is the best compliment. The person whose compliment was not chosen takes the center chair for the next round.

You can vary this by placing the person who will receive the compliments in the center to choose the two who will compliment her, and then replace her with the person whose compliment she likes best.

Content Survey

Sunday school is a prime opportunity for spiritual growth, yet is usually the least popular of junior high church events. This can be turned around by giving junior highers a say in determining the content for their Sunday school. The following survey on page 84 will give your junior highers ownership of the Sunday school content.

CONTENT SURVEY

Circle the ten topics that interest you most.
Star (★) three of the ten you would most like to learn about.

Abortion
Alcohol and Drugs
Angels, Demons
Authority, Government
Balanced Lifestyle
Basics of
    the Christian Faith
The Bible:
    How to Study It
Books of the Bible
Careers
Cheating
The Christian Life
Christian Vocations
The Church
Communication Skills
Community
Criticism: How to Stop
    Chopping People
    Down
Cults
Current Events
Dating
Death and Dying
Discipleship
Discipline
Divorce
Doubt
Drinking
End Times
Entertainment/Media
    (Movies, TV, Music)
The Environment
Evolution vs. Creation
Exercise, Diet
Faith
Family
Fear
Feelings
Fellowship
Forgiveness
Friendship
Gambling

Genesis—Old Testament
    book
God
God's Promises to Us
Gossip
Guilt
Hard Teachings of Jesus
Heaven
Holiness
Homosexuality
Jesus
Leisure Time
Life of Christ
Love
Lust
Lying
Making My Life Count
Materialism
Missions
Money
My Future
New Testament:
    An Introduction
Nuclear Power
Obedience
The Occult
Old Testament:
    An Introduction
Other Religions
Parents: How to Relate
    to Them
Partying
Peace or War
Peer Pressure
Perseverance
Prayer
Prejudice
Preparing for
    High School
Prophecy
Proverbs—
    Old Testament book
Psalms—
    Old Testament book

Rebellion against God
Relationships
Revelation—
    New Testament book
Rock Music
Satan
Self-Image
Sermon on the Mount
Servanthood
Sex
Sin
Smoking
Spiritual Battles
Spiritual Gifts
Sports
Suicide
Surviving School
Temper
Temptation
Truth: Is the Bible
    Really True?
Who's Who
    in the Bible, or
    God's Hall of Heroes
Work/Summer Jobs
World Concerns
Worry/Depression
Worship

Your Body:
    God's Temple
Your Future
Zits

Other:

_____

_____

_____

_____

_____

_____

_____

_____

_____

_____

_____

84

Create an Open Climate

Helping junior high students deal with the tremendous surge of positive and negative feelings they experience is essential for healthy growth, because most kids will deal with their feelings in one of three ways:

They will *take it out,* creating turmoil with their parents, themselves, friends, youth workers, or their teachers.

They will *hold it in,* creating future emotional problems.

They will *talk it out,* creating emotional health and opportunities for growth.

The following ideas will help your junior highers "talk it out" with you.

- Take time to talk with kids before and after meetings. The more you can talk with kids on a casual basis, the more they will begin to trust you.

- Have your kids take time to write down their feelings on particular issues anonymously. As kids write down their feelings, they are one step closer to verbalizing those feelings.

- Use videos of other kids talking about their crises. When kids hear other kids talking openly and honestly about their problems, it helps them to open up more. *Edge TV* (Youth Specialties, 1-800-366-7788) does a great job of dealing with issues like loneliness, sexual choices, racism, self-esteem, and much more.

- Share your own struggles in appropriate ways. We can either impress kids or bless kids, but we can't do both. Too often we try to appear like we have it all together, driving a wedge between us and the kids. There is a tension for us in how to appropriately share ourselves. A good rule of thumb is that it is usually appropriate to share our pain, not our sins. There is nothing wrong with letting kids know we experience pain, doubts, frustration. They know we sin; we don't necessarily need to go into too much detail. Leading authentic Christian lives does not mean we are perfect, but we do not need to list our sins to the kids in order to be authentic.

Discipleship Groups

Many of your junior highers aren't ready for a discipleship group, but some are. If so, sign kids up to be in "Breakaway Groups." The following factors will ensure the success of these groups:

85

High commitment. Make the requirements clear and let the students know the program requires commitment. This can include requirements like attending each biweekly meeting, preparing their material ahead of time, and so on. The length of their commitment to these groups should be clearly defined. It's best to tie them in to the school calendar (fall semester, spring semester, and a summer group).

Caring leaders. The success of junior high discipleship groups depends on what happens between meetings. Meeting with the students outside of regular meeting times provides consistency and leads to success.

Prayer partners. Each junior high student is given a prayer partner to pray for and with. Change partners every two weeks.

Action-oriented content. We charged the students a small fee to attend the group, bought workbooks with the money, and used these workbooks as the content for the meetings. We also built in Scripture memory exercises. Both of these worked best when I met with the students between meetings and we did the preparation work together.

In addition to the number of quality discipleship workbooks available on the market, you can use the five "Breakaway" studies on pages 87–91 to help your junior highers take "action steps" in the area of encouragement.

BREAKAWAY

A Junior High Discipleship Study Sheet
Title of study: Operation Encouragement
Read the Scripture; then answer the study questions and take the action step(s).

MEETING: *1*   SCRIPTURE: *Romans 12:9-21*

STUDY QUESTIONS	ACTION STEP
What commands are given in this passage?	*Pick the verse that grabs you most from this section. Write it here.*
What does this passage teach about love?	*Write one specific step you can take to fulfill this command.*
Which of these will be toughest for you to do?	

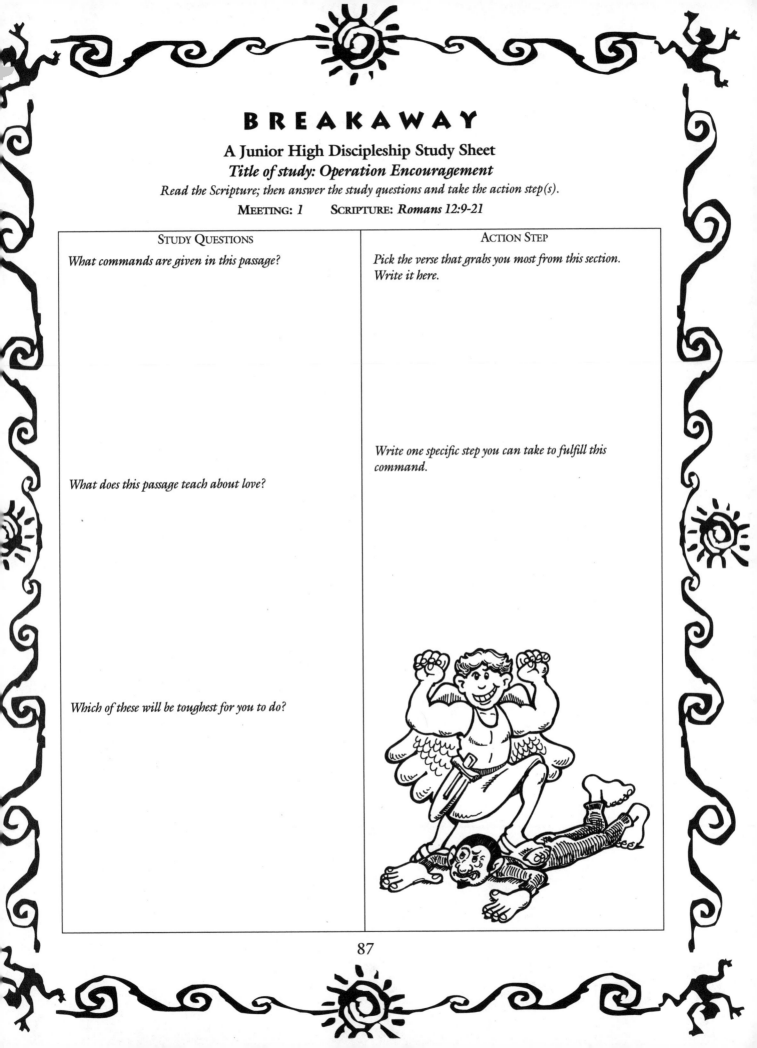

87

BREAKAWAY

A Junior High Discipleship Study Sheet
Title of study: Operation Encouragement
Read the Scripture; then answer the study questions and take the action step(s).

MEETING: *2*   **SCRIPTURE:** *Galatians 6:1-10*

STUDY QUESTIONS	ACTION STEP
What does this passage say about our friendships?	*Write and send a note within the next two days to an adult in your church who has encouraged you.*
What do you think "bear one another's burdens" means?	
Who is a person that has done that for you?	

BREAKAWAY

A Junior High Discipleship Study Sheet
*Title of study: **Operation Encouragement***
Read the Scripture; then answer the study questions and take the action step(s).

MEETING: 3   **SCRIPTURE: *I Corinthians 13***

STUDY QUESTIONS	ACTION STEP
List the characteristics of a loving person in this passage.	*Circle the one quality that you would most like to have describe you. Pray that God would develop that in your life.*
What does this say about the importance of love?	

B R E A K A W A Y

A Junior High Discipleship Study Sheet
Title of study: Operation Encouragement
Read the Scripture; then answer the study questions and take the action step(s).

MEETING: 4   **SCRIPTURE:** *Acts 4:36, 37; 9:26, 27; 15:36-40*

STUDY QUESTIONS	ACTION STEP
What was Barnabas's nickname?	List a person here who has been an encouragement to you.
	Call that person within the next two days and say thanks.
What do you learn from Barnabas about giving?	
List all the ways you can find that he encouraged others.	
What do you learn from Barnabas about loyalty?	

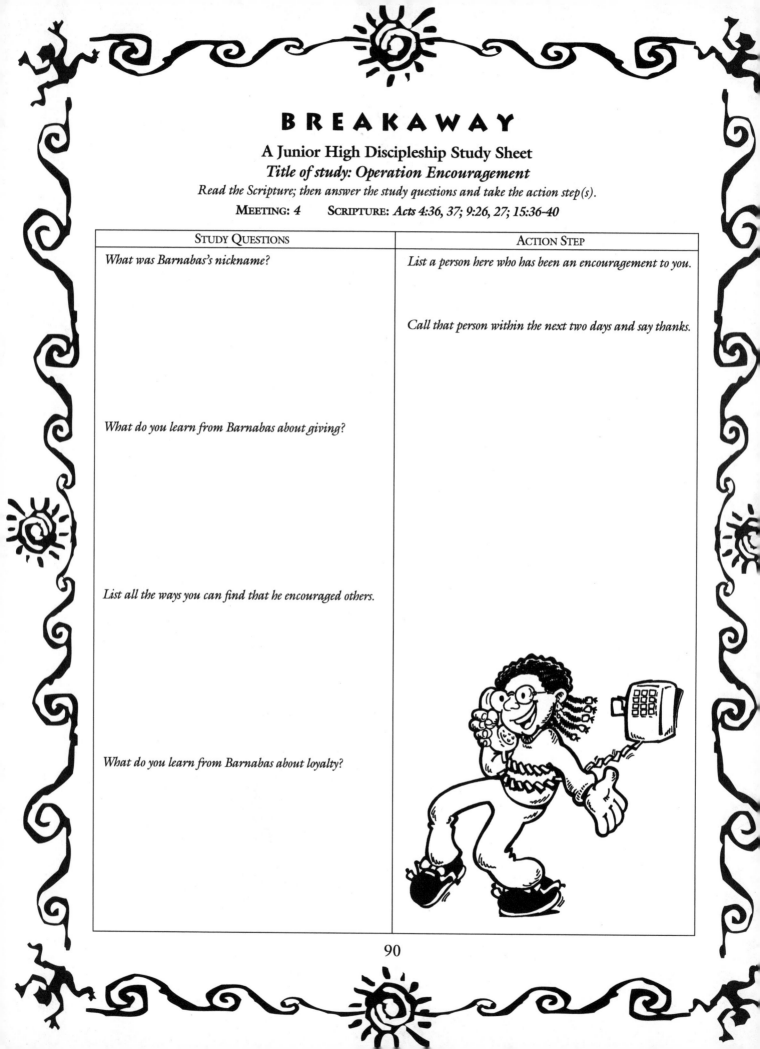

BREAKAWAY

A Junior High Discipleship Study Sheet
Title of study: Operation Encouragement
Read the Scripture; then answer the study questions and take the action step(s).

MEETING: 5   **SCRIPTURE:** *Mark 2:1-12*

STUDY QUESTIONS	ACTION STEP
How did the four friends encourage their friend?	*Write the names of three friends you would like to bring to Jesus.* *1.* *2.* *3.* *Take a minute and pray for a way to encourage each of these friends.*
What obstacles did they have to overcome?	
What was Jesus' response to their faith?	
Who has "carried" you during tough times in your life?	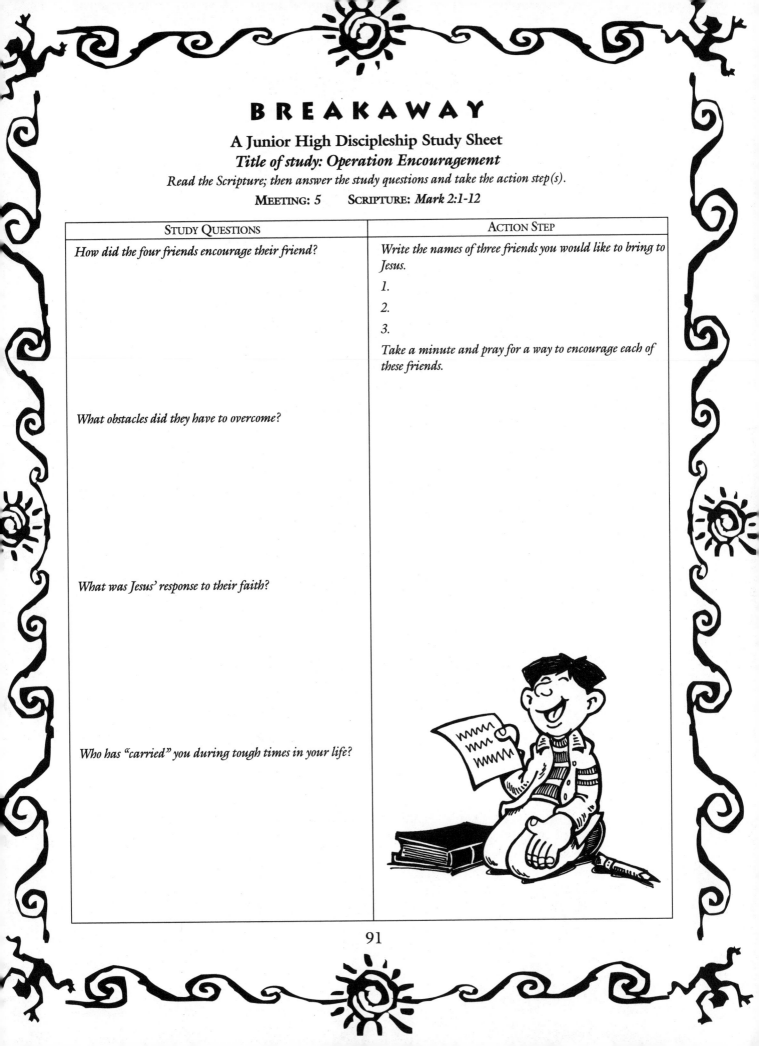

Pray with Your Junior Highers

When students are going through tough times, a great way to minister to them is to pray with them. This teaches your kids about prayer, models a life of prayer, and helps students to know you care. After talking with a student, I will often ask them if they mind if I pray for them. With their permission, I will pray for them right there. Whether this occurs on the phone or in a corner after a meeting, students know that God and I both care.

Praying with your junior highers in groups can be surprisingly exciting. Some of the best prayer times I have had in groups have occurred when I have allowed kids to share prayer requests at a retreat and then opened the group up for prayer. It is often easier for students to ask God to help their friends than it is for those students to tell their friends that they care.

Relationships with Volunteers

Linking students and volunteers will enhance your follow-up and kids' spiritual growth.

First, assign specific students to your volunteers. The minute a student walks in for the first time, they will "belong" to someone. In my junior high ministry, I used this "Adult Volunteers" chart and prayed like crazy while recruiting a volunteer for each spot.

ADULT VOLUNTEERS		
6TH GRADE	7TH GRADE	8TH GRADE
Guy's Volunteer	Guy's Volunteer	Guy's Volunteer
6TH GRADE	7TH GRADE	8TH GRADE
Gal's Volunteer	Gal's Volunteer	Gal's Volunteer

Volunteers who know which kids are "theirs" will do a much better job of making sure these students receive care. That keeps kids from slipping through the cracks.

Second, give your volunteers a job description that helps them to develop relationships. If you ask for two hours per week per volunteer for relationship building, design a job description that fleshes that concept out, such as this:

15 minutes per week to write an encouraging note to a kid

15 minutes per week to phone kids

30 minutes per week to grab a coke before or after a meeting

1 hour per week to lead your junior high kids in a small-group Bible study

This will allow your volunteers to be consistent even with busy schedules. I would tell potential volunteers that I don't want a lot of their time, but I do want 100 percent commitment for two hours per week. Kids deserve an adult who will be there for them.

Secret Spiritual Sponsors

To give your junior highers affirming relationships with adults in your church, create a Secret Spiritual Sponsor (or Adopt a Junior Higher) program where adults in the church are asked to sponsor (or "adopt") a teenager in your junior high group. They commit to support that young person with their prayers, birthday cards, notes of encouragement, and other appropriate, meaningful ideas. Give sponsoring adults an information card on "their" youth (see sample card on page 94); the cards are reminders as well as a source of information. At the end of the school year, organize a secret sponsor appreciation banquet as a "thank you" to those adults. Introduce the teenagers to their sponsor and have them sit together at the banquet. A great follow-up service idea is to have the teenager sponsor a younger kid at the church for the next year.

Secret Spiritual Sponsor
Information Card

Name: *Larry B—*

Address: *1000 Dodger Lane*

City: *Beverly Hills, California*

Phone: *123-4567*

Birth date: *9/16/80*

Friends: *Mark and Scott Johnston, Gary Black, Tony Collins, Scott Shaull*

Hobbies: *Waterskiing, basketball,* Sports Illustrated

Comments: *Larry is a seventh grader at Suzanna Shores Junior High School. Parents are Jesse and Ginger, members of our church; they moved here five years ago from Milwaukee. Has brother Joe and sister Carol. Dad played major league baseball and Larry loves the Dodgers.*

PLACE
PICTURE
HERE

Secret Spiritual Sponsor
Information Card

Name: _____

Address: _____

City: _____

Phone: _____

Birth date: _____

Friends: _____

_____

Hobbies: _____

Comments: _____

_____

_____

_____

PLACE
PICTURE
HERE

Such Good Friends

An important part of spiritual growth is helping students think about their friendships. Relationships are of primary importance to most junior highers. To help kids think through friendship, ask them to answer each of the following questions on their own before discussing them with the group. (See the "Such Good Friends" sample sheet on page 96.)

SUCH GOOD FRIENDS

1. What is friendship? How do you define it?

2. Why do we need friends?

3. Describe the perfect friendship.

4. Describe a lousy friendship.

5. List some of the qualities of a successful friendship that the following verses suggest:

   I Samuel 18:1; 19:1-7

   Job 2:11-13

   Proverbs 17:17

   Proverbs 27:5, 6

   Ecclesiastes 4:9-11

   Mark 2:1-5

   John 11:33-36

6. In what ways is God a very special friend? Read the following verses for ideas:

   John 15:13

   Romans 8:38, 39

   I Peter 5:7

   Hebrews 13:5-8

7. Answer these questions for each of your three closest friends.

   _____

   Friend 1

   Name:

   Why he or she is my friend:

   What I contribute to our friendship:

   How our friendship could improve:

   _____

   Friend 2

   Name:

   Why he or she is my friend:

   What I contribute to our friendship:

   How our friendship could improve:

   _____

   Friend 3

   Name:

   Why he or she is my friend:

   What I contribute to our friendship:

   How our friendship could improve:

Volunteer Coupon Book

This idea is great for building positive relationships between junior highers and their volunteers. Create a coupon book that offers a variety of services to the young people and is redeemable any time during the year (see pages 98 and 99). Think up as many coupons as you like, type them up, and put them together in a book. Volunteers can give these to any kid they think needs one. Coupons can include the following:

- Good for one free dinner at my house.
- Good for one free talk session (void between 11:00 p.m. and 7:00 a.m.).
- Good for prayer for any prayer request.
- Good for one free ride to a local destination of your choice (within reason).
- Good for one encouraging word. Redeemable any time.
- Good for one free pat on the back when needed.
- Good for one pretty good answer to your most burning question.
- Good for one treasure map: a free treasure will be given to anyone who visits the youth pastor's office Monday through Friday between 9:00 a.m. and 4:30 p.m. Call for an appointment.

These coupons not only offer the junior highers something for free, they also make them aware of the kinds of things you're willing to do for them.

FREE! • FREE! • FREE! • FREE! • FREE! • FREE! • FREE! • FREE!

FREEBIE COUPON!

To _____

FROM _____

Good for one free

_____

No expiration date.
Coupon must be submitted at time of use.

FREE! • FREE! • FREE! • FREE! • FREE! • FREE! • FREE! • FREE!

IT'S ON US!

To _____

FROM _____

Good for one free youth group outing to

_____

No expiration date.
Coupon must be submitted at time of use.

FREE! • FREE! • FREE! • FREE! • FREE! • FREE! • FREE! • FREE!

FREE SODA!

To _____

FROM _____

Good for one free soft drink at

FAST FOOD RESTAURANT _____

No expiration date.
Coupon must be submitted at time of use.

FREE! • FREE! • FREE! • FREE! • FREE! • FREE! • FREE! • FREE!

FREEBIE COUPON!

To _____

From _____

Good for one free

_____

No expiration date.
Coupon must be submitted at time of use.

FREE! • FREE! • FREE! • FREE! • FREE! • FREE! • FREE! • FREE!

LET'S EAT!

To _____

From _____

Good for one free dinner at my house

_____

No expiration date.
Coupon must be submitted at time of use.

FREE! • FREE! • FREE! • FREE! • FREE! • FREE! • FREE! • FREE!

FREE RIDE!

To _____

From _____

*Good for one free ride to a destination
of your choice (within reason)*

Destination _____

No expiration date. Coupon must be submitted at time of use.

CONCEPTUAL IDEAS

CREATIVE LEARNING EXPERIENCES

Junior highers love to play games, and it stands to reason that any content that you can put in learning game form is going to be more effectively communicated to junior highers. The following are examples of how you can create games or experiences to communicate spiritual truth.

Electric Fence

This game can be played just for fun, or you can debrief the experience with the group afterward to learn more about how your kids work together to solve problems.

Divide into teams of ten or less, and have each group perform the following task separately. Tie a string or rope about five feet off the floor between two poles or objects. The object of the game is for the entire group to get over the string ("the electric fence") without touching it. Other rules: no one can go under the fence or around the fence, and no one is allowed to touch the poles or objects the string is tied to. In most cases, the group will have the most difficulty with the last persons over the fence.

Foot Washing Experience

This learning exercise helps junior highers have a meaningful experience in humility and service. Begin by reading John 13:1-17. After the reading, discuss questions like these with the group:

- Why did Jesus wash the disciples' feet?
- Why was foot washing a custom in those days?
- Who usually did the foot washing in those days?
- How do you think the disciples felt when Jesus washed their feet?
- How would you feel if Jesus washed your feet?

After the discussion, divide into groups of four or five. Give each group a water-filled dishpan and towels. Allow each group to take turns washing each other's feet. Encourage them to do it in the same spirit as Christ did when He washed His disciples' feet.

Following this experience, ask the group to reflect on what happened: How did this make you feel? Which was most difficult? Washing? Being washed? How can we symbolically wash each other's feet on a regular basis?

Fifteen Ways to Get Kids Talking

Kids love to talk (just check their parents' phone bill), and discussion is an effective way to get kids interacting with your content. The following ideas are great ways to get kids talking:

- Start with nonthreatening questions.
- Begin with questions that ask for opinions.
- Instead of starting with a question, begin with a roleplay, case study, or tension getter that provokes a response.
- Give your opinion about a subject and ask kids to respond.
- Ask kids to anonymously write down their responses to a question or topic. Collect their papers to read aloud; then let the kids respond to what they wrote.
- If the group is large, divide into smaller groups to discuss the issue; then have each group report their conclusions to the larger group.
- If the group combines kids of varying ages (twelve year olds with sixteen year olds, for example), divide into discussion groups of similar ages.
- Ask the kids why they are not talking; discuss their responses to that question.
- Make the dialogue seem more like a game with discussion starters like *TalkSheets,* available from Youth Specialties, or *Talk It Up!* from the *Incredible Meeting Makers* series by David C. Cook.
- Play a round-robin game with discussion leaders. Students take turns asking the questions that keep discussion moving, as well as responding to other kids' comments.
- Brainstorm all the possible responses to the question.
- Ask all adults to leave the room while the kids discuss the questions on their own. When the time limit is up, the adults return to hear the kids' report on what they discussed.
- Give the kids a survey; discuss the results.
- End the meeting formally; then informally bring up some of the issues of the discussion.
- Forget the discussion this time and try it some other time.

Five-Minute Topic Tapes

A great way to make information on tough topics available to junior higgers is to develop a tape library. Make cassette tapes of yourself, your pastor, and/or a professional Christian counselor discussing specific "tough topics" with practical suggestions on what to do. Possible topics include the following:

- Can I commit a sin that even God can't forgive?
- I can't get along with my parents.
- I don't want to live anymore.
- I'm not doing well in school.
- I may have a sexually-transmitted disease.
- I may have been sexually abused.
- How do I know that God is real?
- How do I know what God's will is?
- How far is too far on a date?
- I don't like the way I look.
- My parents are getting a divorce.
- What do I do if I'm pregnant?
- What do I do when nobody likes me?
- Where will I go when I die?
- Why should I wait until marriage to have sex?

Each one of these tapes should be short, five minutes at the most. You can also add on to the tape the testimony of a teenager who has dealt with that issue. Put the tapes where they are easily accessible, and label the tapes so the kids know what they are about. Arrange your check-out system so that kids can take tapes anonymously; replace missing cassettes with a duplicate.

You can enlarge this idea into a comprehensive audio/video/CD library for your kids. Talks by great youth communicators and good Christian music provide your kids opportunities to get Christian perspectives on issues.

Scripture Search Scavenger Hunt

This scavenger hunt is not only fun, but it gets kids into the Bible as well. To discover the items that must be brought back, the kids need to look up the verses and answer the questions. Use this list or create your own!

1. Luke 15:8—A woman had ten of something. You bring the same. (10 coins)

2. Matthew 16:19—Jesus said He would give Peter something. Bring one back. (a key)

3. Revelation 11:1—Bring in something we use today like the thing John was given. (measuring instrument)

4. Mark 14:20—Jesus dipped bread into something. Bring one in. (dish)

5. Isaiah 24:12, 13—Bring back one of the two things you could eat. (olive or grape)

6. Matthew 5:13—Bring in what Jesus says we are. (salt)

7. I Peter 2:2—Bring in some of the beverage found here. (milk)

8. Hebrews 1:9—God has set you above your companions by anointing you with the _____ of gladness. Bring any kind. (oil)

9. Matthew 4:3—Bring in what Satan dares Jesus to turn stones into. (bread)

10. James 1:11—Something falls off. Bring one in. (flower)

Spiritual Growth Notebooks

Invest in some three-ring binders and give (or sell) them to your kids to use as spiritual growth notebooks. You can include sections for the youth group calendar, the youth group roster, prayer, Bible studies, songs, message notes, handouts, articles, work sheets, and journaling. Students bring the notebooks to youth meetings and discipleship groups. A fun way to make these look sharp is to buy the three-ring presentation binders with the slot on the front for inserting graphics, then insert a group picture or colorful group logo.

Spiritual Growth Progress Chart

This chart is adapted from Mike Rowe, former youth worker at Trinity Baptist Church in Nashua, New Hampshire. Faced with a youth group that was quickly growing in numbers, he wanted to come up with some means by which he could continue to track the individual spiritual growth of each student. To help in this regard, he developed the following chart for each student in his group. He placed a + in each area where that student was progressing well, an 0 in each area where that student was stagnant, and a - in each area where that student was especially struggling.

SPIRITUAL GROWTH PROGRESS CHART

Student's Name _____

Phone _____ Birthday _____ Year of Graduation _____

Area of Growth

Walk with God

Devotional Life

Understands that God loves him or her .... _____

Is getting to know the Bible......................... _____

Is starting to apply God's Word .... _____

Has a consistent time with a positive adult .... _____

Is developing a prayer life .... _____

Doctrine

Is beginning to develop a working knowledge of the following:

Scripture... _____

God... _____

Jesus Christ .... _____

Holy Spirit .... _____

Sin and salvation .... _____

Assurance of salvation........................ _____

The importance of the church............. _____

Daily Life

Is developing a positive self-image
based on God's love .... _____

Life is motivated by a biblical understanding
of justification (not by guilt) .... _____

Demonstrates understanding of
submission to God's Word......................... _____

Has a few goals and is beginning
to know what is important .... _____

Uses time well .... _____

Fellowship

Has a love for God's people .... _____

Builds healthy relationships .... _____

Demonstrates compassion and servanthood.. _____

Beginning to understand spiritual gifts......... _____

Is committed to a local church.................... _____

Evangelism

Is actively seeking to share Christ
with friends .... _____

Has been taught how to share the Gospel..... _____

Has shared the Gospel with someone........... _____

Has shared his or her testimony
with a friend or group .... _____

Has a working knowledge of
basic apologetics...................................... _____

Teach Using Different Styles

Not all people learn in the same way. Some learn primarily through their feelings, others by watching or listening, some by thinking, some by doing. See the list below for a list of teaching strategies, organized by learning style. The next time you are communicating to junior high students, experiment with methods from each of the categories.

Learn by			
FEELING	WATCHING & LISTENING	THINKING	DOING
game show	chalkboard	agree/disagree	field trips
pantomime	maps	debate	question & research
write a rap	interviews	flannelgraph	panel discussion
advertisement	overhead projectors	case study	dramatization
brochure	video of Bible story	field trips	roleplay
songwriting	storytelling	option play	video of Bible study
paraphrase a hymn	children's books	questioning	game show
make banners	photography	research	simulation games
bumper stickers	laser show	inductive study	video
simulation games	acrostics	tension getters	let them teach
collage	memory work	apologetics	camps and retreats
badges	outlining	guest speakers	learning games
coat of arms	test taking	leader vs. student	dialogue
murals		debates	
discussion			
posters			
letter writing			
poetry			
diary/journal			

Use Illustrations and Stories

For most junior highers, listening to an adult lecture ranks up there with homework as something they like to avoid. However, kids love stories and great illustrations, most of which effectively communicate the point we are trying to make. I have found the following resources to be a great source for stories and illustrations.

Slivers from the Cross, Brad Hill, Covenant Press

Ragman and Other Cries of Faith, Walter Wangerin, Harper San Francisco

The Ragmuffin Gospel, Brennan Manning, Questar

The Applause of Heaven, Max Lucado, Word

God Came Near, Max Lucado, Questar

No Wonder They Call Him the Savior, Max Lucado, Questar

Joan 'n the Whale, John Duckworth, Baker

All I Really Need to Know I Learned in Kindergarten,
   Robert Fulghum, Vilard Books

Hope for the Flowers, Trina Paulus, Paulist Press

The Millionaire and the Scrublady, William Barton, Zondervan

The Lemming Condition, Alan Arkin, Harper San Francisco

The Wall, Eve Bunting, Clarion Books

The Runaway Bunny, Margaret Wise Brown, Harper Collins

The Sneetches, Dr. Suess and other stories as well.

Incredible Stories, Tom Finley, Youth Specialties

Hot Illustrations for Youth Talks, Wayne Rice, Youth Specialties

ACTION IDEAS

EXCITING WORSHIP EXPERIENCES

All it takes is one trip to a rock concert to realize that junior highers have a great capacity for worship. The problem is that adults seldom worship God in a style even remotely exciting to a kid. You may want to try some of the following ideas to help increase your kids' capacity to fall in love with Jesus.

Praise/Adoration/Thanksgiving

• Write honest thank-you notes to God.

• Give God a standing ovation. Compose cheers.

• Write psalms of praise/thanksgiving.

• Thanksgiving Exchange. An exercise in which junior highers list some things that they know another person in the group can be thankful for.

• Thanksgiving Graffiti. Kids write what they are thankful for on a large sheet of paper in a well-traveled part of the church.

• Creation Meditation. Junior highers meditate on Scriptures read from Genesis 1.

• Quaker Worship Service. Worship where kids participate as they feel led by the Holy Spirit. Works great at camps or retreats.

Singing Hymns and Spiritual Songs

- Make good use of new worship music. Play good Christian music with slides in the background and let the students meditate on the words.
- Paraphrase traditional hymns. Kids can restate the messages of hymns in everyday language.
- Read the words to hymns responsively.
- Use dance, movement, and motions to enhance the music.
- Use rhythm instruments when appropriate.
- Let students rewrite hymns to contemporary music.

Confession/Absolution

- Give kids opportunities to confess their faith, confess sin, pray, receive sacraments (for example, Communion) in other ways: writing, small group sharing, creative arts, media, etc.
- Conduct a "Service of Reconciliation" where the kids in the group ask forgiveness from those they have wronged and forgive those who have wronged them.
- Symbolically forgive sin by having kids write them on paper and then lighting a match to the paper in a container, a trash can, or nailed to a cross.

Personal Bible Study

Helping junior highers learn to study the Bible for themselves is critical for future spiritual growth. The most helpful tool that I have used with kids was taught to me by my youth pastor, Chuck Miller, now President of Barnabas Ministries. Using the acrostic PROAPT, he taught us to *Pray* for God's insight; *Preview* the passage; *Read* the passage; *Observe* what it's saying; *Apply* the lessons learned; *Pray* for personal application, and *Tell* someone what you learned.[3]

Post-Retreat Resolutions

A great way to attempt to build consistency in the lives of junior high kids is to build on the decisions they have made at camp. You may want to let them choose one of the following post-camp options:

- Write your parents a letter of affirmation.
- Clean up your room for a week without being asked.
- Be at the youth group for three weeks in a row.

- Sit in the front row at church for a month.
- Clean the entire house while your parents are gone.
- Write a friend an encouraging letter.
- Wash your parents' car inside and out.
- Give five dollars to a worthy cause.
- Memorize five Bible verses.
- Write your folks a long letter telling them what happened this week/weekend on our retreat.
- Teach your dad how to record programs on the VCR.
- Ask a counselor to meet weekly with you to be your spiritual coach.
- Write a letter to yourself stating some personal commitments you have made as a result of your camp/retreat experience. Put the letter into a sealed, self-addressed stamped envelope and give it to your youth leader. Ask him or her to mail it to you a month later to remind you of your commitments.

Progressive Worship Service

Here's a fun way to involve your junior highers in worship. It can be done in a church, in homes, or on a weekend retreat. There really is no limit to its possibilities. It works just like a progressive dinner.

A worship service has a variety of elements, just like a dinner does. By taking each element of worship separately and in a different location, it provides a good opportunity to teach young people about these elements of worship. Acts 2:42 and Colossians 3:16 provide a good scriptural base. Here's one way to do it:

1. *Fellowship:* At the first location, begin with some kind of group interaction and sharing that provides a chance for the kids to get to know one another better. Something that would put the kids in a celebrative, but not rowdy, mood would be appropriate.

2. *Spiritual Songs:* At the next location, have someone lead the group in a variety of well-known songs of worship. If your group doesn't sing well, you may want to substitute a slide show to music.

3. *Prayer:* Move to another location that provides a good atmosphere for prayer. If outside, a garden can be nice, as Jesus often chose a garden for prayer. Have the kids offer prayer requests, thanksgivings, etc., and have several kids lead in prayer.

4. *Scripture Reading:* At the next location, have several kids read passages from the Old and New Testaments. Use a modern English translation.

5. *Teaching:* The next stop can be where a brief message is given. If you prefer, you can deliver a message without being "preachy" by using a dialogue sermon, a film, or some other alternative. Location can make this an unforgettable experience, for example, a sermon on materialism with the kids in a junkyard.

6. *Breaking of Bread (Communion):* The last stop can be around the Lord's table, with a communion service. Conduct this however you choose, but it should be a time of celebration and joy.

There are other ingredients that go into worship (like the offering), which you can incorporate into the others or take separately. Design your own progressive worship service, and you can be sure that your group will never forget it.

Risk-Taking Events

For many junior highers, becoming a Christian and taking steps of spiritual growth is a risk. They risk ridicule, unpopularity, and the loss of established friendships. Putting kids in environments where they take physical risks can help students be more comfortable taking spiritual risks. Some fun ways to do this include the following:

- *Wilderness trips*—a great time to think and reflect
- *Rock climbing* (with trained professionals leading)
- *White water rafting*—great for risk taking and community building
- *Ropes Courses*—many camps and retreat centers now have high and low courses
- *Make up your own.* At my last water-ski retreat, we took students to a ten-foot-high rope swing at midnight. Kids held on, swung out over the lake, and let go for a ten-foot free-fall into the lake in total darkness. It was a blast, created great memories, built community, and gave us the opportunity to teach. We were able to point out the necessity of letting go of things that were keeping us from trusting God.

These adventures, while scary at first, give the kids a sense of accomplishment and competence when they are finished.

Ten-Minute All-Night Prayer Meeting

All-night prayer meetings are not very common with most junior high youth groups these days. In fact, they aren't all that common, period. But they can be very meaningful and effective, especially for the participants. The problem with long prayer meetings (for most people) is endurance, or lack of it, and the fact that it is difficult to pray for more than two or three minutes at a time, let alone two or three hours. But this idea—The Ten-Minute All-Night Prayer Meeting—just might be the answer.

Here's the format: The prayer meeting starts at midnight. This could be a gathering of the committed kids in your group following a youth group activity, a concert, or other event. They should be adequately prepared—that is, aware of the need for "continuous" prayer and of the power of prayer. A Friday night is ideal.

Take your kids to different areas around your city. At each site they then spend ten minutes praying for the people related to that location. Go to each local junior high school and pray for their friends and teachers. Next, go to each of the students' homes and pray for their families, parents, brothers, and sisters. This type of prayer meeting holds student interest and builds community while giving students a heart for their friends and a rare nighttime adventure.

Workbooks

In the realm of learning, discovery is always preferable to declaration. Retention and interest are higher and the student leaves with a higher confidence level that he can learn. Using discovery-oriented workbooks is an excellent way to get junior highers studying the Scriptures for themselves. Books like *Living Your Life as God Intended* (Jim Burns, Harvest House) and *Junior High School TalkSheets* and *More Junior High TalkSheets* (Youth Specialties) are outstanding for enabling students to learn for themselves. I have used these books and others like them individually and in groups. Give the students a few minutes to work on the workbook, then pull them together and let them share what they've learned.

Youth Celebration Night

Many junior highers love the youth group and hate the church. That combination spells trouble for long-term spiritual growth. Here's a great way to help your junior highers develop appreciation for the whole church. Our Youth Celebration Night is an annual event hosted by the youth group. We invite the whole church to a Sunday night carnival that includes a dunk tank, food for sale (hot dogs, etc.), games, music, student testimonies, a slide show recap of the year, and the introduction of our summer program. At the end of the evening, the kids in the youth group thank their youth workers and present them with small gifts of appreciation. It's a wonderful way to affirm your volunteers publicly and to allow your students to "star" in front of the whole church. For many of our junior highers this was their first experience with the whole church. Many of them liked it and got involved at deeper levels after this evening.

WHAT YOU HOPE TO ACHIEVE

Junior high spiritual growth experiences can be fun, memorable, meaningful, unpredictable, and life-changing. The potential gains are numerous. Some of the gains you will be able to pray for and expect as your students grow spiritually include the following:

Confidence in Christ. Giving junior highers a relationship with a God of grace and with adults who consistently affirm will produce confidence and self-esteem. Students will know they are loved, forgiven, accepted, and affirmed. What greater gift could a junior higher receive?

Healthy values. As students get to know the Bible, it will shape their values. With the average American's values being shaped by the media, helping our junior high students examine those values in light of Scripture is critical in helping them to form solid, biblical standards.

Excitement. Kids are apathetic when they are spectating. Action-oriented opportunities and good relationships break through this apathy, and students become motivated as they take advantage of these opportunities.

Healthy relationships with caring adults. Too many junior high kids are segregated from everyone but other junior high kids. Being included in the life of the church, having a secret spiritual sponsor, and having their own affirming volunteer gives your students far more levels of relationships than most junior highers enjoy.

Better friendships. Students who pray together, learn to affirm each other, and share similar convictions will develop close relationships. This type of support system will serve them well as they seek to live out their faith.

Strength against temptation. Kids growing up in today's world are faced on a daily basis with decisions regarding sex, drugs, alcohol, and cheating. Spiritually growing students will acquire the spiritual and relational resources they need to face and overcome temptation. For some, that may make all the difference.

Staying focused on these and other benefits will help keep you encouraged as you build real-life growth into your junior high students.

GATEWAYS: LEADING JUNIOR HIGHERS ON TO SERVICE

In my own youth ministry experience, getting kids involved in missions and service took them to new levels of growth and stability. Students who made the transition developed a fresh love for God and eventually became the leaders of our high school ministry. The obvious benefits of helping students cross this bridge make building this gateway a high priority.

The following gateway strategies are designed to help you move your students from being spectators to participants. Some are simple, while others will take considerable setup; but the benefits of each will be worth it.

Eighth-Grade Leadership Team

This is a great way to capitalize on the eighth graders' past experience and keep them excited about your junior high ministry. We had a monthly meeting, structured ministry teams (welcome team, camp planning team, ski retreat team, publicity team, etc.), and required the leaders to be at each meeting. Not only did this improve our junior high ministry, but seventh-grade students looked forward to joining these groups when they arrived in eighth grade. (For more specific ideas, see the progressive responsibilities principles detailed in Chapter Eight.)

Have Your Key Students Sign Up Early

Whenever we were attempting to build momentum for a mission trip or service project, we "primed the pump" by having some of our key students, like the eighth grade leadership team, sign up prior to announcing the event. We could then announce that we had only a certain amount of spots left. This created the atmosphere that the event was going to be "hot," and fringe students were motivated to jump in.

Linking Events

A great way to help students make the jump to service is to link your outreach/growth events to service events. This will affect the order of your special events. In our ministry, we had two major events during the second semester. In January, we sponsored an outreach ski retreat, followed two months later by a mission trip. At the end of each ski retreat, we showed slides and students gave testimonies about the mission trip. This "linked" the two events and increased the possibility of students attending both events. This proved to be a great way of helping students move quickly into service.

Parent Support

As we mentioned in Chapter 6, parent support for any significant spiritual growth step is critical. Each year, when recruiting students for a missions trip in Mexico, I knew that the determining factor in any junior higher's ability to attend was the permission of his or her parents. Prior to announcing the event, we had a parents' information meeting where we detailed the trip, showed slides from the previous year, had students share the benefits of their experience, gave information about handling homework and teacher permission, talked about scholarship help, and took questions and answers. A little encouragement with some parents can go a long way in securing support for taking students on significant trips.

Prayer Tour of the Inner City

A great way to teach compassion and give your students an experience where prayer is taken seriously is to take a prayer tour of the inner city. Assemble your junior highers in your church van and drive around the inner city. Pause in front of spots you've preselected for your kids, talk about the circumstances and needs of the people, and lead a short time of prayer while they're in the van. You could stop in front of

- a skid row hotel
- a group of prostitutes on the corner
- a soup kitchen for the homeless
- a rescue mission
- the county hospital
- the police station

This experience will build community, teach kids to pray, and give them a heart for people who hurt.

Students Service Project Pre-Trip

Taking a couple of key students on a preliminary trip to your service project can be a great motivator for the rest of your group. These students will spread the word about the needs to the rest of your group, and the rest of the students will be much more likely to join.

113

CHAPTER SEVEN

Three-Step Strategy

Paul Borthwick, in his book *Youth and Missions* (Victor, 1988), suggests a three-step strategy for getting students involved in missions and service: example, exposure, and experience. Students will be more motivated to experience missions and service if we have exposed them to the needs of a given situation. Speakers, slide shows, videos, or your own testimony will touch the hearts of your junior highers and motivate involvement in your mission trip or service project.

Endnotes

1. Robert Laurent, *Keeping Your Teen in Touch with God* (Chariot Family Publishing, Elgin Ill., 1988), 1.

2. Dennis Miller, "Christian Teenagers: They're Leaving the Flock," *Moody Monthly,* September 1982.

3. Chuck Miller, Barnabas Ministries, P.O. Box 1358, Lake Forest, Calif. 92630.

Creating Service Opportunities for Junior Highers

HAVING SPENT A CAREER TRYING TO UNDERSTAND and help young people, I am convinced that the one primary cause of the tragic self-destruction of so many of our youth is that they do not know the work and satisfaction of living for something larger than themselves. The human psyche cannot stand up against moral neutrality. If nothing is truly good, right, and worth striving and sacrificing for, life is meaningless and no course of action can build a sense of one's own self-worth. Without large goals, life is barren, life is a burden.

—John A. Howard, past president
of the Rockford Institute
in *The Rotarian,* July 1989

ROBERT FULGHUM, AUTHOR of *All I Really Need to Know I Learned in Kindergarten* (which I unfortunately read after seminary), has a perceptive observation about the lack of passion in the lives of people as they grow older:

Ask kindergartners how many can draw—and all hands shoot up. Yes, of course we draw—all of us. What can you draw? Anything. How about a dog eating a fire truck in a jungle? Sure? How big do you want it?

How many of you can sing? All hands. Of course we sing. What can you sing? Anything. What if you don't know the words? No problem, we can make them up. Let's sing. Now. Why not?

Try those same questions on a college audience. Only a few of the students will raise their hands when asked if they draw or dance or sing or paint or act or play an instrument. Not infrequently, those who do raise their hands will want to

115

qualify their responses—I only play piano, I only draw horses, I only dance to rock and roll, I only sing in the shower.

College students will tell you they do not have talent, are not majoring in art or have not done any of these things since about third grade. Or worse, that they are embarrassed for others to see them sing or dance or act.

What went wrong between kindergarten and college? What happened to "Yes! Of course I can"?

—*Newsweek's* Special Issue on Education
(Fall/Winter 1990)

Giving junior highers opportunities to serve keeps their passion alive as they discover that they can meet needs and make a difference. Junior high students are capable of serving in almost any capacity if we match the service to their potential.

In my last youth ministry, we designed a service/fund-raising project called Operation Serve. Students volunteered to work on a Saturday for eight hours and raised money for each hour worked. The projects involved every kind of community service imaginable. Students worked in convalescent homes, cleaned an inner-city day-care center, took blind people shopping, and cleaned cages at the humane society. Some of the students served our church by painting and cleaning the homes of several elderly people in our congregation. The money raised went to support missions.

Operation Serve became a yearly tradition in our church. Over six years, our junior highers met many needs in our community and gave thousands of dollars to missions. Junior high kids can and do make an impact when they are given the right opportunities.

In this chapter, you'll find ideas for setting goals, anticipating gains, and developing your game plan for getting your junior highers involved in service. The chapter concludes with "gateway" ideas to help your junior highers make a healthy transition into high school.

POSSIBLE GOALS

Effective goal setting in the area of service will take into account both attitudes and actions. The key in setting goals is to balance optimism and realism. Setting positive goals enables you to help your students grow by trying things they might not have considered. Being realistic keeps you from setting unreachable goals and causing discouragement. Keep in mind your junior highers' maturity and experience levels, and attempt to stay one step ahead of your kids.

Here are some goals you can consider.

- Introduce junior highers to the needs that exist around the world.
- Introduce junior highers to the needs that exist in large cities.
- Develop the concept of authentic Christian response to needs.
- Provide opportunities for junior highers to learn about world hunger.
- Help junior highers discover that they are gifted and enable them to act on that discovery.
- Provide opportunities for junior high kids to serve their local communities for a day.
- Provide opportunities for junior highers to go on short-term mission trips.
- Help junior highers see themselves as a legitimate part of the church.
- Help junior highers serve in real roles that enable them to contribute to the church.

GAME PLAN IDEAS

RELATIONAL IDEAS

Adopt a Grandparent

This service project is great for junior highers who are mature enough to make a relatively long-term commitment. First, take the entire group to visit a convalescent home or the homes of elderly people in your church who live alone. You may want to sing, put on a play, or bring cookies to break the ice. Allow the kids to mingle with these people, so that they get to know them better.

Afterward, introduce the idea of adopting one or more of these seniors as a "grandparent." Each young person would be assigned (or would choose) one or two elderly people to visit on a regular basis and to remember on special occasions. The "adoption" should continue for a specific period of time—perhaps six months to a year or longer, depending on the kids.

The youth sponsors would monitor the program and offer help and encouragement to the kids who are involved. One junior high group in suburban Illinois has built this program into their Sunday school. Every other week during the Sunday school hour, the whole group goes to the convalescent home to visit their adopted "grandparents." Most junior highers find this to be a very rewarding experience, and the elderly people involved will appreciate it greatly.

Big Brother/Big Sister Program

Your eighth-grade junior highers may want to become big brothers or sisters to the younger students coming into your youth group. This could be as simple as having your big brothers and sisters get to know the younger kids by name and make a point to welcome them each Sunday at church. Other ideas include having big brothers and sisters invite them to youth group events, visit them at their homes, or send them encouraging notes. It's helpful to meet monthly with the big brothers and sisters to see how they are doing and to encourage them to stay faithful in helping their younger brother or sister. This idea is a wonderful way for your older junior highers to be positive role models for younger kids.

Come Play for a Day

Our church sponsors a program that gives junior highers the opportunity to develop positive relationships with kids in the inner city. The first Saturday of each month, our junior highers gather at the church, materials in hand, and head to an apartment complex in the inner-city. There, they set up a play-oriented Vacation Bible School. Kids in the complex know they are coming and come out of the woodwork. Our junior highers benefit from the ministry, and the mothers of the kids in the complex love the program.

Eighth-Grade Servant Teams

A great way to encourage relationships between your older junior highers and younger ones is to create servant teams. Organize your teams, select a monthly meeting time for planning and encouragement, and let your kids apply for one of the teams. You can offer the following options, or create your own teams.

Welcome Team

A. Welcome people to youth group by saying hi and talking with them.
B. Collect visitor cards, divide them up, and write each new person a thank-you card the following week.

Operation Encouragement

A. Organize refreshments for selected events.

B. Bring food and an inexpensive present to celebrate the birthdays of everyone in the group.

Reach Out and Touch Someone

A. Call new or "fringe" people and invite them to youth group events.

B. Call everyone in the group to invite them to special events.

These types of involvements help eighth-grade students contribute to the youth ministry, feel significant, and prepare for involvement in leadership when they enter your high school group.

Get out of Jail Free

A youth group in Massachusetts sponsors a monthly ministry to the parents in the community that they have named Get out of Jail Free. On the first Saturday night of the month, they provide free baby-sitting and child care at the church. Some of the junior high students staff the church nursery and the rest put on a Vacation Bible School for the older kids. The service is free and the whole evening is planned, staffed, and run by the youth group. The only requirement is that the parents go out on a date. This is a great idea for building positive relationships with young couples and their kids.

Homeless Guest Speaker

Bring in a homeless person from a local rescue mission as a guest speaker for your youth group. Allow the students to interact with questions and answers about his or her background, life on the street, and hopes and dreams. For many kids this will be their first face-to-face encounter with need and may result in new understanding and action.

Junior High Sponsor Search

Many adults are afraid to work with junior high students because they are afraid the kids won't like them. A great way to counteract this and start student-adult relationships off on the right foot is to get your junior highers involved in the process of recruiting and selecting adult sponsors. Teaching students to find people who can build them up develops their ability to find those types of people in the future. The following idea is a practical way to put that plan to work.

Begin by surveying your junior highers about the potential sponsors in your church. Ask questions like the following:

1. Which of the college students and adults in this church do you most like?
2. Which of the adults do you most respect?

Compile the list, agree with the students on choices, write your expectations for volunteers, and then have students contact and recruit the potential sponsors.

Sandwich Ministry

Every Friday afternoon in Chicago, youth worker Sean Bloomquist and his kids make two hundred sandwiches and head to needy sections in Chicago where they give out these sandwiches to the homeless. They often return to the same places, which provides opportunities for relationships to develop. This is a great way to enable junior highers to put a face to the problem of homelessness.

Sponsor a Child

A great way to get junior high students involved in world relief programs is to encourage them to sponsor their own needy child. Agencies like World Vision and Compassion International link financial sponsors with children overseas. Usually, these agencies will ask for a certain amount of money each month to provide food, clothing, and shelter for a particular child. Most of the time, you will receive detailed information about your child, including photos and handwritten thank-you notes from the child. The monthly cost to sponsor a child is usually the price of one large pizza and a movie.

If the sponsorship is too expensive for one student, have your junior high group adopt one of these children. Each person in the youth group can give a certain amount (like $1.00 per month), and the child's progress can be monitored by the entire group. The group can also pray for the child on a regular basis. Not only is a project like this easy to do, but it helps junior highers develop an awareness of, and compassion for, world needs.

Vacation Bible School

The most valuable relational service experience for my junior highers has been involvement in VBS. Students are good at it because many of them have been in it as kids and know how it runs. Students build positive relationships with people of all ages because they are working with kids and alongside adults. The average Christian education director is desperate for help and thankful beyond words for the junior high students' assistance.

We encouraged involvement by cancelling most of the junior high meetings during the summer VBS and announcing the VBS job openings in all of our meetings. Junior high students are capable and available, and this experience is a great way to develop their relational and leadership abilities.

CONCEPTUAL IDEAS

Congratulations! You Are Gifted!

With the disease of insecurity running rampant in the lives of most junior highers, a study on spiritual gifts may be just what the doctor ordered. I have found the following three learning activities and resources valuable in helping junior highers discover that they are uniquely gifted and definitely needed.

- The first resource is *Up Close and Personal* by Wayne Rice (1990, Youth Specialties). This thirteen-week community-building curriculum contains an excellent section on spiritual gifts, complete with work sheets and a leader's guide for each work sheet. Well written, balanced, and easy to use, this is the best resource I have found for giving kids positive relationships and helping them discover that they have gifts.

- Another idea for building students' knowledge of their gifts and abilities is the *strength voting exercise*. This activity affirms kids by helping them see their strengths through the eyes of others.

  Ask kids to write their names at the top of a sheet of paper, as well as three things about themselves that they consider to be their strengths. Warn them against excessive modesty. If they think they're good at something, tell them to be honest and write it down (for example, good listener, sense of humor). You may want to pre-write the first one on each kid's sheet.

  When your kids are finished listing their virtues, ask them to pass the sheets around the room so that others in the group can "vote" on the strengths listed for each person. As the sheets make their rounds, kids should mark a check by those qualities that they agree are prominent strengths. If anyone thinks that an obvious top-three strength is missing from someone's list, he or she should write in that strength. All of the sheets should end up with lots of check marks and some write-in votes.

When kids get their own papers back, they'll have a fairly clear idea of which strengths others see in them. Follow this up with a study on spiritual gifts and the call to service.

• To help kids understand that they are gifted, have them take the "Discover Your Spiritual Gifts" test found on page 123. This test can't be flunked. Follow it up with affirmation. Also have kids brainstorm specific ways they can use their gifts.

DISCOVER YOUR SPIRITUAL GIFTS

The test you can't flunk!

Instructions: *For each question, enter the number that most applies to you.*

3 = *That's Me!*   2 = This is *probably* me.   1 = *Definitely not* me!

___ 1. I try to think more about the needs of others than my own.

___ 2. People come to me when they need to talk out a problem.

___ 3. I have given money to those in need.

___ 4. I don't mind being seen with people who aren't that popular.

___ 5. When I see needy people on cold nights, I really feel like inviting them to my home.

___ 6. On Friday nights, I am usually the one who decides where we go and what we do.

___ 7. I like to invite my friends to church.

___ 8. I have confidence that God will get me through both good and bad times.

___ 9. I like doing jobs that most people don't want to do.

___ 10. I am known for my positive attitude.

___ 11. I get a real kick out of giving stuff away.

___ 12. I would like to work with disabled people.

___ 13. I like having friends stay overnight at my house.

___ 14. I like to organize and motivate groups of people.

___ 15. I can sometimes make discussions relate to God.

___ 16. I believe that God can do things that seem impossible.

___ 17. I have helped other people so their work was easier.

___ 18. I like to help sad people feel better.

___ 19. I try to be smart with my money so that I can give extra money to people who need it.

___ 20. I feel very sympathetic toward the needy.

___ 21. I like having guests at my home.

___ 22. I have encouraged others to get better grades.

___ 23. I would like to help someone else become a Christian.

___ 24. I have confidence that God will keep His promises even when things are bad.

___ 25. I don't mind doing little jobs that other people don't consider important.

___ 26. I can encourage others through what I say.

___ 27. I know that God will meet my needs, so I want to give freely to others.

___ 28. If a friend is sick, I call to see how he or she is doing.

___ 29. I like having company come to my house.

___ 30. I would like to help people who are homeless.

___ 31. I would like to tell others that Jesus is the Savior and help them see the positive results.

___ 32. I trust that I can call on God and know that He will be there when "impossible" situations happen.

___ 33. Sometimes when I do jobs, nobody notices, but I don't mind.

___ 34. I like it when people are happier after I have talked to them.

___ 35. I have given away my money or belongings to those in need.

___ 36. When I see a homeless person, I really want to help.

___ 37. My friends come over to my house because they feel comfortable there.

___ 38. When I'm in a group, sometimes people look to me to take charge.

___ 39. I take any opportunity I can to tell people about Christ.

___ 40. When everything looks bad, I can still trust God.

DISCOVER YOUR SPIRITUAL GIFTS

Tabulation

Instructions: 1. *Put your response (1 to 3) to each test question in the blank next to the appropriate number on the chart below.*

2. *Add up the numbers going across the blanks and record them in the box under "Total."*

Test Question Number: Your Response					Total	Gift
1:	9:	17:	25:	33:	=	A
2:	10:	18:	26:	34:	=	B
3:	11:	19:	27:	35:	=	C
4:	12:	20:	28:	36:	=	D
5:	13:	21:	29:	37:	=	E
6:	14:	22:	30:	38:	=	F
7:	15:	23:	31:	39:	=	G
8:	16:	24:	32:	40:	=	H

Explanation

GIFT A: *Helping.* The ability to assist and serve other people.

GIFT B: *Encouraging.* The ability to support people and help them to regain hope.

GIFT C: *Giving.* The ability to give your time and money so that it can be used for God's work.

GIFT D: *Mercy.* The ability to act compassionately toward those who are suffering.

GIFT E: *Hospitality.* The gift of being friendly and generous to guests.

GIFT F: *Leading.* The ability to motivate others to use their spiritual gifts and to do their best for the work of the Lord.

GIFT G: *Evangelism.* The ability to help others to come to know Jesus personally.

GIFT H: *Faith.* The ability to have a confident belief that God will always do what is the very best.

Assessment

Determine your demonstrated, probable spiritual gift(s) as follows:

If the score in the "Total" section is

10-15: There is great evidence that God has blessed you with this gift.

7-10: There is a good possibility that God could be developing this gift in you.

3-6: You are spiritually gifted in areas other than this one.

Have a Lockout

Instead of locking the junior high kids in the church overnight, lock them out of the church. Restrict them to a controlled area on the church grounds. Have boxes for them to sleep in, fire barrels or barbecues for them to keep warm around, and one (*only* one) chemical toilet on the grounds for their use. Do not provide running water.

Arrange for people in your church to drive up and feed your kids a meal out of the back of their cars. After the meal, let the kids experience a night out in the cold. You can plan a Bible study by flashlight related to God's concern for the poor.

Have your kids discuss their experience the next morning before they depart for home.

Thirty-Hour Famine

This is a weekend "lock-in" type of event that builds awareness of world hunger through a planned famine/fund-raiser. The event begins with a Friday night simulation dinner, during which some of the students eat steak, some eat rice, and some eat nothing. The three groups are selected totally at random. Students then fast for the next twenty-four hours while learning about world hunger. The junior highers then collect the money they have raised and give it to world hunger. This project is available from World Vision (919 West Huntington Drive, Monrovia, CA 91016).

Luxury Taxes

Most American junior highers have more stuff than ninety-eight percent of the rest of the world. The following activity (on page 126) is a great way to balance the scales. Do a little scavenger hunt to figure out how much stuff your kids have, then levy "luxury taxes" as follows:

```
_____ 10¢ for each pair of shoes you have/5¢ extra for each pair of Air Jordans
_____ 25¢ for every movie you have seen in the last month
_____ 10¢ for every TV in your house
_____ 50¢ if you have a TV in your room
_____ 15¢ for every VCR in your house
_____ 50¢ if you own your own stereo system (25¢ extra if you have a CD)
_____ 10¢ for every car your family has
_____ 25¢ if you have your own car
_____ 25¢ for every watch you own
_____ 75¢ if you have a job or get an allowance
_____ 25¢ if you have ever called Dominoes and ordered a pizza
_____ 10¢ for each album or CD you own
_____ TOTAL AMOUNT
```

Have each kid total his or her sheet; then collect the money and donate it to a reputable relief agency or local charity. Close with prayer that God will use the money to make a difference in the lives of those whom it will help.

On-Site in a Cancer Ward

Learning outside the classroom is particularly effective with junior highers. This idea, from *On-Site* by Rick Bundschuh (Youth Specialties) is great for giving junior highers a look at their priorities. Believing that most of the people in this world have their priorities backwards and that it often takes a brush with death to make a person reevaluate what is important, Bundschuh recommends taking junior highers to a cancer ward in a hospital. You might consider combining your lesson with some sort of service project in the hospital. Ask the nurses for ideas; they often know what would be most helpful. Obviously, you'll need to clear your plans ahead of time with hospital officials.

Be sure to explain to your students what type of behavior you expect from them. Ask them to try to put themselves in the place of the patients. If you can't take your students into the hospital itself, just sitting on the grass outside the hospital can still have an impact.

Getting Started. Before leaving for the hospital (and before you have informed your students where you are going), ask your group, "If you just had a physical examination and the doctor said 'There is something I need to talk to you about,' what would be your greatest fear?" Their responses may be varied, but very likely someone will mention a disease that has the potential to be terminal. When they've completed their responses, explain where you're going and the purpose of the lesson.

Looking in the Word. Bible passages to share and discuss: Matthew 6:33, Hebrews 9:27.

Begin your lesson by sharing the idea that many people, when faced with a potentially fatal illness, reevaluate what is really important in life. Have your students examine the passages you select and then create a list of priorities in life that are dictated by Scripture.

Plugging In to Daily Life. Ask your students to create a double list: on one side, what people usually live for; on the other side, what they might live for if they were faced with imminent death. Contrast the values represented in the two columns.

Adding It All Up. Ask your students to imagine that they were diagnosed as having cancer, and that they knew they had only a short while to live. Have them write letters to their friends and families, expressing what would be important to them if they really faced imminent death.

People Shopping

Here's a scavenger hunt that will strengthen your junior highers' concern and awareness of others.

Take your group to a shopping mall to "people shop." Your kids go from store to store and observe people, following instructions on a "shopping list" you give them. The shopping list instructs the kids to go into specified stores, select individuals in each store to observe for a minute or two, and then answer these questions:

1. Why did you choose this particular person?
2. What can you learn about this person by what they're wearing?
3. How does this person make you feel?
4. Do you think you could be friends with this person?
5. How do you think this person feels right now?

At the end of the "people shopping," bring your kids back together and have them share their experiences, describing the people they observed. Emphasize the importance of noticing other people, caring about how they feel, and empathizing with them. Close by praying for all those who were observed during the activity.

Service Bible Study

The "You Can Help" work sheet on page 129 is designed to help junior highers interact with scriptural principles of giving. Depending on your junior highers, this could be used in a weekend format or in weekly growth groups. Photocopy and distribute the study to every student. This is probably best done with the students. You can hold each other accountable for the action parts of the study.

YOU CAN HELP!

Read the following verses and write what you think each has to say about people who are hurting.

WHAT DO THESE VERSES SAY ABOUT PEOPLE WHO ARE HURTING, HUNGRY, POOR, AND SICK?
Matthew 25:34-40
Acts 2:44, 45
Acts 11:27-30
Romans 12:13

Which of the following would you be most excited about doing in order to make a difference in a hurting world? Fill in each of the blanks with a number ranking them from 1 (most concerned) to 5 (least concerned):

_____ Pray for victims of hunger and poverty.

_____ Pray for people at my school who seem to be struggling.

_____ Support a Compassion child.

_____ Go on a mission and service trip with the junior high group.

_____ Go to the city with our youth group to learn about the needs there.

_____ Meet with kids at the local juvenile hall.

_____ Talk as a youth group about a project we could do to alleviate world hunger.

_____ Help plan a service project in our community.

Now the fun starts. Pick one of the above ideas that you rated the highest and write a specific action step or steps in the box below.

ACTION STEPS

Sleep in a Box

Take a supply of cardboard boxes with you on your next junior high camp or retreat. At some point during the event, have your kids spend one night sleeping in a box, with nothing but their clothes and perhaps an old blanket for warmth.

The next morning, have your group discuss what it felt like to live, for one night, like the thousands of homeless people living in boxes all over America.

The Compassion Project

A great way to bring the world into your church is to use good programs that deal with the themes of hunger and starvation. *The Compassion Project,* from Compassion International (P.O. Box 7000, Colorado Springs, CO 80933-7000) is a good example of this kind of tool. Utilizing simulation games, video, music, Bible studies, and discussion starters, this project offers several different avenues to approach servanthood. The best news is that it's free!

Another outstanding release from Compassion is the new twenty-eight minute video, *XTREMES*, a high-quality production detailing the reaction of kids upon traveling to South America to meet children they sponsor through Compassion. This video is also free.

Urban Scavenger Hunt

In my last church, the junior highers knew nothing about the world of the inner-city. To introduce our students to the city, we held an Urban Scavenger Hunt. We took our junior highers to an inner-city church where we were to spend the night. During the late afternoon we broke them into scavenger hunt groups (each with an adult sponsor) and gave each a list of items, each worth different amounts of points. The scavenger hunt included items like these: Buy three non-English speaking newspapers and get the headlines translated; get directions to the city hall; buy three types of food you have never heard of, etc. We met back at the church and wrapped up the evening by sampling all of the new food that they had bought. This gave them the opportunity to get into the inner-city and observe for themselves the sights, sounds, and smells of this other world so close to home.

Visit an Inner-City Church

Take your junior high kids to a Sunday service in an inner-city church. These churches can range from small storefront congregations to large sanctuaries that hold thousands of people. Your kids will have the opportunity to rub shoulders with Christians from a different culture and experience a church service that will be quite unlike what they're normally used to. Discuss the similarities and differences between the congregations and the services with your kids on the ride home.

ACTION IDEAS

DEVELOPING PROGRESSIVE RESPONSIBILITY IN JUNIOR HIGHERS

Junior high students are ready for responsibility in varying degrees. Responsibility is developed by handling responsibility. Some kids are only ready to set up chairs while others are ready to work with people. Use the chart on page 132 to identify your students' ability levels and match them with appropriate jobs. Write your students' names at the bottom of the chart and then brainstorm which tasks they can handle.

CHAPTER EIGHT

Developing Progressive Responsibility in Junior Highers

PHASE 1	PHASE 2	PHASE 3
Physical Responsibility	*Program Responsibility*	*People Responsibility*
EXAMPLES		
Set up chairs Set up projectors Load luggage Hand out flyers Arrange transportation Count the offering Break out of jail after counting the offering	Plan the program Do the welcome Lead songs Lead games Give testimonies Play in student band (get earplugs) Teach in VBS Design and present the youth budget	Outreach team Big brother/big sister to younger kids 8th-grade encouragers Birthday celebrations Operation Encouragement Lead a Bible study Be a part of the missions trip team
KIDS		
Ted Smith Dave Fredrickson Tim Ek Evelyn Johnson Kyle Becchetti Richard Rice Wayne Long Kitty Kelly	John Wyper Michele Veal Ilene Perryman Andrea Aronstam Steve Schibsted Scott Benson	Carrie Wyper Bill Laffin Bernie Ogden Jill Hall Michelle Ogden Melissa Ogden

PHASE 1	PHASE 2	PHASE 3
Physical Responsibility	*Program Responsibility*	*People Responsibility*
EXAMPLES		
Set up chairs Set up projectors Load luggage Hand out flyers Arrange transportation Count the offering Break out of jail after counting the offering	Plan the program Do the welcome Lead songs Lead games Give testimonies Play in student band (get earplugs) Teach in VBS Design and present the youth budget	Outreach team Big brother/big sister to younger kids 8th-grade encouragers Birthday celebrations Operation Encouragement Lead a Bible study Be a part of the missions trip team
KIDS		

Inner-City Mission Weekend

Tired of the typical camp? Take your students to do hands-on ministry in the inner city. They may never recover from this powerful experience of serving and education. One of the best organizations for making the most of this opportunity is the Center for Student Missions. Students are led by trained staff into the city and work alongside a variety of inner-city ministries. Weekend or week-long trips are available. I have observed firsthand the change in the lives of junior highers entering this program.

Center for Student Missions

P.O. Box 900 • Dana Point, CA 92629

(714) 248-8200

Ministries: VBS, Children's ministry, Food Distribution, Shelter ministry

Time Span: Customized

Mission Field: Inner-city Los Angeles, Chicago, Washington, D.C.

P.S. Most parents are extremely nervous about letting their kids go on this type of trip. CSM has a video you can show to the parents before beginning to promote the trip. It's available for five dollars from CSM.

Mission Trips

Every Easter, I spend a week in Mexico with 4,500 teenage missionaries, many of them junior highers. For them, the opportunity to serve God and experience another culture is a life-changing experience. The following organizations specialize in taking teenagers on mission trips, and *all of them take junior high students.* You may want to contact them for details.

Adventures in Missions

ATTN: Seth Barnes

6629 Forest Hill Blvd. • West Palm Beach, FL 33413

(407) 790-0394

Ministries: Construction

Time Span: One to two weeks

Mission Field: U.S. and Latin America

Institute of Outreach Ministries

Azusa Pacific University

901 E. Alosta Ave. • Azusa, CA 91702

(818) 969-3434

Ministries: VBS, children's ministry, evangelism

Time Span: One week

Mission Field: Mexico

SIMA/Mission to the World

P.O. Box 29765 • Atlanta, GA 30359

(404) 320-3259

Ministries: Construction, VBS, evangelism

Time Span: Two weeks

Mission Field: Worldwide

101 Ways to Choose a Leader

Many junior high youth groups elect a president, vice president, and other "standard" officers. That works well in some settings, but may leave most of the students feeling unpopular and uninvolved. *101 Ways to Choose a Leader* is a great way of involving junior highers in the youth group who would not otherwise sign up for leadership, while eliminating competition for leadership roles. Try any that look like fun next time you need help with the junior high group.

1. The person who has visited the most states in America.
2. The person from the largest family.
3. The person whose birthday is closest to the youth pastor's.
4. The person who is seated closest to the youth pastor.
5. The person who has never been to Disney World/Land.
6. The person who lives farthest from the church.
7. The tallest person.
8. The person with the smallest shoe size.
9. The person wearing the most blue.
10. The person who has used the most modes of travel (boat, car, train, plane, etc.)
11. The person in your group who loves spinach the least.
12. The person wearing shoes that don't lace.
13. The person with the darkest hair.
14. The person who weighed the least at birth.
15. The person who stayed closest to home on his or her last family vacation.

16. The person who has been to church camp the most weeks.
17. The person who has used an outhouse the most number of times.
18. The person with the least number of letters in his or her full name.
19. The person with the most first cousins.
20. The person who has had the most boyfriends/girlfriends.
21. The person who has made the most A's in school.
22. The person who has most recently kissed on the first date.
23. The person who uses Crest toothpaste, or has used it the longest.
24. The person who has to get up the earliest for school or work.
25. The person with the most pets.
26. The person with the biggest hand.
27. The person with the most syllables in his or her full name.
28. The person with the most jewelry on.
29. The person with the youngest sibling.
30. The person who uses Dial soap.
31. The person who lives farthest from a hospital.
32. The person who watched Saturday morning cartoons most recently.
33. The person who has worn braces the longest.
34. The person whose family has the oldest model car.
35. The person who has eaten most recently.
36. The person who has attended the most professional basketball games.
37. The person who has had the most broken bones.
38. The person who has been to the dentist most recently.
39. The person with the most vowels in his or her full name.
40. The person with the youngest mother.
41. The person with the most buttons on.
42. The person who got the least amount of sleep last night.
43. The person who learned to ride a bicycle at the earliest age.
44. The person who has the most older siblings.
45. The person who learned to swim at the youngest age.

46. The person who has eaten at the most fast-food restaurants in the past week.
47. The person with the most dental fillings.
48. The person who has been in the most car accidents.
49. The person with the most M's in his or her full name.
50. The person who has been shopping most recently.
51. The person whose birthday is closest to Groundhog Day (Feb. 2).
52. The person with the shortest hair.
53. The person who was the longest at birth.
54. The person to go on vacation most recently.
55. The person with the most uncles.
56. The person who has never kissed on a first date.
57. The person from the smallest family.
58. The person with the largest shoe size.
59. The person with the lightest hair.
60. The person who has never flown, or who has flown the least.
61. The shortest person.
62. The person who lives closest to a hospital.
63. The person who has visited the fewest U.S. states.
64. The person whose birthday is closest to Jesus' birthday (Christmas).
65. The person who weighed the most at birth.
66. The person who has had the braces off his or her teeth the longest.
67. The person who ate the most for breakfast this morning.
68. The person who ate most recently at McDonald's.
69. The person who can play the most musical instruments.
70. The person who learned to ride a bicycle at the latest age.
71. The oldest person.
72. The person who gets up the latest for school or work.
73. The person with the smallest hand.
74. The person with the fewest syllables in his or her full name.
75. The person whose birthday is closest to today's date.

76. The person with the most grandparents living.
77. The person with the oldest sibling.
78. The person who most recently purchased an album.
79. The person who has had the most part-time jobs.
80. The person who has lived in the most houses or apartments.
81. The pickiest eater.
82. The person who watched the most TV in the past week.
83. The person who has traveled the farthest around the world at any one time.
84. The person with the most letters in his or her full name.
85. The person who has had the most stitches.
86. The youngest person.
87. The person with the most younger siblings.
88. The person who lives closest to his or her school.
89. The person who is wearing the most red right now.
90. The person with the most black on.
91. The person who got the most sleep last night.
92. The person with the most S's in his or her full name.
93. The person with the longest little finger.
94. The person with the fewest vowels in his or her full name.
95. The person with the youngest father.
96. The person whose family owns the smallest car.
97. The person with the most aunts.
98. The person who went away the farthest on his or her last vacation.
99. The person who was shortest in length at birth.
100. The person with the longest hair.
101. The person with the most letters in his or her first, middle, and last names.

Saturday Servants

To give your kids a regular chance to serve church members with special needs, designate occasional Saturday mornings (9:00 a.m. to noon) as the time for "Saturday Servants." Use a bulletin insert announcing the project two weeks before your event, so church members who need assistance can call the church ahead of time with their requests.

"Saturday Servants" focus primarily (though not necessarily exclusively) on performing chores for the elderly, shut-ins, widows, divorced persons, and single parents in the church. Jobs to be done might be anything from yard work to child care, car maintenance to furniture moving. It's a good idea to ask the people being served to provide the necessary equipment and cleaning supplies, if possible.

Your youth will find that their sacrifice of time and energy on a Saturday morning can provide a significant and practical ministry to many members of the church.

Service Scavenger Hunt

Throw tradition into "reverse" for this scavenger hunt. Instead of collecting a list of items, as in a regular scavenger hunt, this one allows the kids to give. Each team of scavengers is given an identical list of service projects to do. The list could include the following: wash ten windows, mow one lawn, raise ten dollars for a Compassion kid, etc. Each project is worth a given amount of points. Teams score points by completing the projects (under the supervision of an adult sponsor). The team with the most points wins. Junior highers will have a ball and will have served the community at the same time.

Smoke Alarm Ministry

The irony of smoke alarms is that the elderly, who need them the most because it takes them the longest to get out of the house, are the least able to install the alarms. Junior highers in your youth group can install smoke alarms for elderly people in your community who cannot or will not climb up on a ladder to install one. Sometimes fire departments are even willing to give the smoke alarms to the youth group if the youth group will install them. The end result is a tangible, lifesaving ministry.

Student-Led Mission Experience

Many of us struggle with our junior highers wanting to go to Disneyland to play, but not to Mexico to work. A great way to overcome apathy and motivate students to get involved in missions and service is to give them ownership of the project:

1. Place the majority of the decision-making responsibility for the experience into the hands of the students. Let them select the project (from a prescreened list), plan the time, transportation, supplies, finances, etc. When students get to shape an event, they tend to sign up immediately.

2. Place the majority of the program work responsibilities into the hands of the students. Let them decide the details, write the schedule, and organize the work at the site. Under your supervision and guidance, they usually do a good job of carrying the ball.

3. Bring the experience home with you. Students who plan and organize a mission and service trip will want to share the results with the world. Schedule times for the kids to report back to the congregation about their trip—a special service, a "Thank You" dessert for financial supporters of the trip, and other opportunities. These times will build the students' self-esteem and the congregation's appreciation for the junior highers.

Taking kids on a mission trip is never easy, but is always worth the hassle. An excellent resource to help you motivate, recruit, organize, finance, and train junior high students for missions is *The Complete Student Missions Handbook,* by Ridge Burns and Noel Becchetti (1990, Youth Specialties).

Work Camps

Another service experience that will have lasting impact on your kids are work camps. Kids will play hard, work hard, and grow from the experience, and parents are sometimes more willing to let a kid go to work camp than to the mission field. The following organizations take junior high students and put them to work in camp settings:

Group Work Camps
2890 N. Monroe Ave.
P.O. Box 599 • Loveland, CO 80538
(303) 669-3836

Ministries: Construction

Time Span: One week

Mission Field: U.S.

Confrontation Point Ministries
P.O. Box 50 • Ozone, TN 37842
(615) 692-3999

Ministries: Home repair, day camps, medical needs ministries

Time Span: One week

Mission Field: Appalachia

CHAPTER EIGHT

Mountain T.O.P.
P.O. Box 128 • Altamont, TN 37301
(615) 692-3999
Ministries: Construction
Time Span: One week
Mission Field: Tennessee

WHAT YOU HOPE TO ACHIEVE

Involvement in service, mission, and leadership gets kids out of their comfort zones and triggers accelerated spiritual growth. Some of the gains you may be able to pray for, and expect from, involvement in service include the following:

Improved self-identity. Giving junior highers involvement at the leadership level of the youth ministry has tremendous benefits in the area of self-esteem. Stanley Coopersmith, in his book *The Antecedents of Self-Esteem* (1967, W. H. Freeman), suggests four essential components to a healthy self-image: significance, competence, power, and virtue. Opportunities to serve give junior highers the sense that they are making a difference (significance); they discover that they have skills (competence); they get to make decisions (power); and responsibility for service develops character (virtue).

Better relationships. The best relationships in my youth ministries developed when kids were working side by side on the mission field. The walls that were up during Sunday school came down on the field.

Discovery of gifts. The average junior high kid watches adults perform at school, at church, on TV, etc. They are convinced that we, not they, are the stars. Involvement in service helps kids discover that they too have gifts that God can use.

A closer walk with God. Kids encounter God in the process of giving their lives away in service. They realize they need God, they hear the call of God, they feel the heart of God. We've had more kids rekindle their love for God in Mexico than in our junior high room at church.

Outward focus. Involvement in service combats self-centered thinking. Junior highers often see the world as a place that exists to satisfy their every want and need. They have been told from day one that they are the center of the universe. Involvement in service awakens them to the fact that they are part of a big world that needs their contribution to it.

Spiritual staying power. Dr. Bob Laurent, in researching his book *Keeping Your Teen in Touch with God* (1988, David C. Cook), discovered that the number-one reason that teenagers dropped out of the church was lack of opportunity for meaningful church involvement. Giving junior highers opportunities to serve in the church helps them feel like a valuable part of the church, making them less likely to leave.

GATEWAYS: MOVING EIGHTH GRADERS TO HIGH SCHOOL

In any relay race, the critical point is the passing of the baton. The race is won or lost during the handoff. The same is true with youth ministry. Helping junior high students successfully make the transition to high school consolidates the gains you have made in junior high.

The following gateway ideas are different from the gateway strategies discussed in Chapters Six and Seven. These gateway ideas are designed specifically to help eighth-grade students make a healthy transition to high school.

Eighth-Grade Appreciation Banquet

This is a great way to say good-bye to your eighth-grade students in an affirming way. Take the last youth meeting in May and turn it into a banquet. Fun decorations, music, pictures of these kids on the wall, and great food will make the evening special. Give a book to each student that has been autographed with notes of appreciation by the other students. Have the evening planned and hosted by your ninth-grade students. This can become a tradition, leaving your eighth-grade students looking forward to hosting the next year's banquet.

Big Brother/Big Sister

At the start of summer, match your incoming high school students with a big brother or big sister from your youth group. Have those big brothers and sisters call their person, write encouraging notes, go get pizza together, and so on. We used this every year, and it made the transition to our high school less fearful. We tried to match students with high schoolers they would attend school with in the fall, so that they knew at least one student from that high school before they hit the campus.

Ninth-Grade Welcome Night

One week after our eighth-grade graduation banquet, the high school group sponsored a Ninth-Grade Welcome Night. We let high school students share what they appreciated about the high school group, played games familiar to the incoming ninth graders, gave out

141

the summer schedule, introduced them to their big brother/sister, and made sure each incoming ninth-grade student was up front at least once. At the end of the meeting, we told them that they were now officially a part of the high school ministry. They now knew they were wanted and were now "officially" a part of the high school group.

Student Search

When you have a new group of ninth graders entering your high school ministry, this event will help them to be welcomed into the group by all the other members.

Deliver all your new ninth graders to various locations around town where they can get lost in the crowd—in a shopping mall, for example, or in a video arcade or playground. The rest of your high schoolers and adult sponsors divide into hunting parties and take off (hunting parties are given a list of the locations) to try to find the ninth graders.

The ninth graders are instructed to blend in with the crowd, but not to run or disappear. It's the job of the hunting parties to recognize them and bring them in.

The catch to this game is that a hunting party just arriving at a location has no way of knowing for sure whether another hunting party has already been there and found the ninth-grader there.

After the game, make sure all the ninth graders have been found; then have a party and award prizes to the hunting party that found the most kids. This activity will help all the kids to get better acquainted and will make the new kids feel accepted and a part of the group right away.

High School Tours

Arrange for tours of the local high schools by the high school students in your group. You may want to go with the eighth-grade students and a high school student to lunch in the cafeteria, then tour the campus. Set up an appointment to meet Christian teachers and other adults on campus who can be encouraging to new students. Contact the school prior to coming and see if they have any material to give to new students that will be helpful.

Guest Speakers

Invite high school kids, Christian teachers, coaches, and/or school officials to speak to your junior highers on "Surviving High School." Invite leaders of local high school parachurch ministries, (Young Life, etc.) to talk about the Christian activities available on campus.

Books and Resources
for Junior High Ministry

Benson, Warren S., and Mark H. Senter III. *The Complete Book of Youth Ministry*. Chicago: Moody Press, 1987.

Borthwick, Paul. *How to Plan, Develop, and Lead a Youth Missionary Team*. Lexington, Mass.: Grace Chapel, 1980.

Bundschuh, Rick. *101 Outrageous Things to Do with a Video Camera*. Ventura, Calif.: Gospel Light/Light Force, 1988.

Burns, Ridge with Noel Becchetti. *The Complete Student Missions Handbook*. Grand Rapids, Mich.: Youth Specialties, 1990.

Campolo, Anthony. *Ideas for Social Action*. Grand Rapids, Mich.: Youth Specialties, 1986.

Campolo, Anthony. *You Can Make a Difference*. Waco, Texas: Word Books, 1984.

Christie, Les. *Unsung Heros*. Grand Rapids, Mich.: Zondervan, 1987.

Clark, Chap. *The Youth Specialties Handbook for Great Camps and Retreats*. El Cajon, Calif.: Youth Specialties, 1990.

Clark, Chap, Duffy Robbins, and Mike Yaconelli. *Option Plays*. El Cajon, Calif.: Youth Specialties, 1990.

Dobson, James. *Preparing for Adolescence*. New York: Bantam Books, 1980.

Hendricks, Howard G. *Teaching to Change Lives*. Portland, Oreg.: Questar, 1987.

Kesler, Jay, ed. *Parents and Teenagers*. Wheaton, Ill.: Victor Books, 1984.

Lynn, David, and Mike Yaconelli. *Grow for It Journal*. El Cajon, Calif.: Youth Specialties, 1985.

Lynn, David. *Junior High Talksheets*. El Cajon, Calif.: Youth Specialties, 1988.

Lynn, David, and Mike Yaconelli. *Tension Getters, Volumes One and Two*. Grand Rapids, Mich.: Youth Specialties, 1981, 1985.

BIBLIOGRAPHY

McNabb, Bill, and Steven Mabry. *Teaching the Bible Creatively: How to Awaken Your Kids to Scripture*. Grand Rapids: Youth Specialties, 1990.

Poling, Debra, and Sharon Sherbondy. *Super Sketches for Youth Ministry*. Grand Rapids, Mich.: Youth Specialties, 1991.

Reichter, Arlo. *The Group Retreat Book*. Loveland, Colo.: Group Books, 1984.

Rice, Wayne, and Mike Yaconelli. *Creative Socials and Special Events*. Grand Rapids: Youth Specialties, 1986.

Rice, Wayne, ed. *Ideas Library*. El Cajon, Calif.: Youth Specialties, 1968 to 1987.

Rice, Wayne. *Up Close and Personal: How to Build Community in Your Youth Group*. Grand Rapids, Mich.: Youth Specialties, 1989.

Rice, Wayne. *Junior High Ministry*. Grand Rapids, Mich.: Youth Specialties, 1987.

Robbins, Duffy. *Programming to Build Disciples*. Wheaton, Ill.: Victor Books, 1987.

Rohnke, Karl. *Cowtails and Cobras 1, Cowtails and Cobras 2*. Project Adventure [Box 100, Hamilton, MA 01936, phone 508/468-7981].

Rohnke, Karl. *Silver Bullets: A Guide to Initiative Problems, Adventure Games, and Trust Activities*. Project Adventure [Box 100, Hamilton, MA 01936, phone 508/468-7981], 1986.

Rydberg, Denny. *Building Community in Youth Groups*. Loveland, Colo.: Group, 1985.

Veerman, David R. *Reaching Kids before High School*. Wheaton, Ill.: Victor, 1990.

Yaconelli, Mike, and Scott Koenigsaecker. *Get 'Em Talking*. El Cajon, Calif.: Youth Specialties, 1989.